Copyright © 2023 by Nicolette Halladay and Inspired Hearts Publishing

All rights reserved. Apart from any fair dealing for the purposes of research or private study, or criticism or review as permitted under the Copyright, Designs, and Patents Act 1988, this publication may only be reproduced, stored, or transmitted, in any form or means, with the prior permission in writing of the copyright owner, or in the case of the reprographic reproduction in accordance with the terms of licenses issued by Copyright Licensing Agency. Enquiries concerning reproduction outside those terms should be sent to the publisher.

ISBN: 979-8-9872110-7-6

Edited by Erin R. Lund, Sunshine Editorial Services & Book Coaching: https://www.sunshineeditorialservices.com/

May you find inspiration among these stories to awaken your own power within!

Sharon

Awakening the Power Within

Inspiring Stories of Transformation & Triumph

Shannon Olsen   Jacquie Fenske   Nichole Walczak

Gina Jenkins   Michelle Seguin   Brandice Scraba

Jennifer A. Telford   Kimberly Stefiuk   Erica Hurtt

Becca Kyle   Belinda Djurasovic   Glenda Sheard

Nicolette Halladay   Taylor A. Caruthers

Contents

Welcome to Awakening the Power Within	vii
1. UNCONDITIONAL SELF LOVE: THE FINAL PUZZLE PIECE IN MY JOURNEY BACK HOME TO MYSELF Shannon Olsen	1
About the Author	11
2. LIVING OUR ANCESTORS WILDEST DREAMS Jacquie Fenske	13
About the Author	23
3. HOW I TRANSFORMED MY BODY FROM AN ENEMY TO AN ALLY Becca Kyle	25
About the Author	35
4. A NEW LENS OF AUTHENTICITY Michelle Seguin	37
About the Author	47
5. NOTES FROM BEYOND Nichole Walczak	49
About the Author	57
6. POSITIVE MIND, POSITIVE VIBES Kimberly Stefiuk	59
About the Author	67
7. THE SOUL SPEAKS TO US THROUGH OUR BODIES: HOW LISTENING TO MY BODY AND SELF-NURTURING LED ME TO TRUST MY VOICE AND OWN MY POWER Jennifer A. Telford	69
About the Author	79
8. LIFE BEYOND HURT Brandice Scraba	81
About the Author	89

9. COMING INTO MY POWER AND FINDING MY VOICE: IT'S NOT ABOUT FINDING THE RIGHT PATH, IT'S ABOUT FINDING THE PATH THAT'S RIGHT FOR YOU Belinda Djurasovic	91
About the Author	101
10. PATTERNS AND POTENTIAL: UNEARTHING CHANGE AT THE BIRTHING CAVE Nicolette Halladay	103
About the Author	111
11. ARE YOU THERE, GOD? I SURE FREAKING HOPE SO. Erica Hurtt	113
About the Author	123
12. DANCING WITH THE DIVINE Gina Jenkins	125
About the Author	133
13. A JOURNEY TO PURPOSE: ON THE WINGS OF COMMUNITY Glenda Sheard	135
About the Author	145
14. AMBITION TO AUTHENTICITY: REDISCOVERING MYSELF ON THE PATH TO EMPOWERMENT Taylor A. Caruthers	147
About the Author	155
Thank you	157
Inspired Hearts Publishing	159

Welcome to Awakening the Power Within

When I was presented with the opportunity to create a multi-author book written by a collaboration of women, I knew I was in for something big and instantly knew what the book needed to be about. I was immediately shown the powerful vision and message this book needed to share and the purpose it needed to serve in the world. I knew the world was in desperate need of more Light in this time of external chaos, fear, despair, and uncertainty all around us. I also knew that I would find an incredible group of women to share in this mission with me, those who were ready to write their story of self-transformation to inspire, motivate, provide hope, and bring Light to those who may be facing challenges, feeling alone, or just needing a powerful spark to re-ignite their own dreams, desires, and belief in themselves to create positive change around them.

I feel to my core that this collaboration of authors is Divinely orchestrated, and I am incredibly grateful and honored to be in connection with these courageous women as we step forward together in empowerment, support, and hope that our stories will touch not only one person but many as we share some of our most vulnerable, yet impactful periods of our lives that have taught us how to see ourselves and life from a different perspective and rise from the ashes of our challenges to witness how our resilience, compassion, and courage can lead us back to the path of our highest potential and truly awaken our power within.

These women are ready for their voices to be heard, and they are sharing their wisdom to help others along their own journeys of uncovering the power that lies deep inside each and every one of us. We all have the ability to transform our lives, and these stories showcase this as we take you with us on our own unique experiences of truly finding ourselves, discovering the core of our existence here, and how we each play a vital role in it.

I hope you enjoy these stories of self-transformation and discovery, and feel a spark ignite within you to dream bigger, stand stronger, and embrace the support and guidance of these extraordinary women as we all unite in shining our Light just a little brighter than we did yesterday.

Let the awakening begin!

In grace and faith,

Shannon

Chapter 1

Unconditional Self Love: The Final Puzzle Piece in My Journey Back Home to Myself

Shannon Olsen

 "Recovering your relationship to self is the greatest gift you will ever give."

~Shannon Olsen~

Had anyone asked me a few short years ago about my relationship to self and the role the state of this relationship played in the unfolding of my life, I would have stared blankly, then quickly recovered and offered this programmed answer: "Oh! I am good with myself, I love self-care practices and I know that it's important to fill my cup first."

LIE.

Ooof, writing that cuts a bit, but it is the truth, and I am done not living in my truth. It was through my journey back to myself that I not only realized WHAT relationship to self is, WHY it is important, and that it is an absolute direct influence in the creation of our lives, but also how it brought about the most crucial piece of all in this shift embodiment: truly living and being authentic, unapologetically authentic and free.

Now let me tell you how I got there and what that roller coaster of a journey looked like…

Was there a time when I thought it impossible to be able to look in the mirror and not let out a token sigh of exasperation as I ran through a list of bodily-improvement to-dos that rattled around daily in my head? Yes. That place of physical perfection definitely felt like a fairytale, like a naïve illusion that was never really attainable. It felt hopeless, like being stuck in a never ending cycle of self-loathing and defeat because no matter what "size" my body was, or what "shape" I was in, it would never be good enough. There would always be "one more thing" to work on, to get rid of, or to fix. THAT was truly rock bottom for me in my relationship to self, the helplessness and despair of realizing that I didn't have the power to get out of this seemingly endless abyss I fell into every time I looked in the mirror. No matter how much I kept transforming my outside, my inside continued to spew toxic thoughts, and the voice in my head continued to taunt me that I would be stuck on this hamster wheel forever. That was when I believed I had no control over my own happiness and that I would be playing a lifetime of chase, self-sabotage, and moving the goalpost each time I got close, because with every moved goal post, there was still no happiness. I was deluding myself into believing that THIS time it would work, and that THIS time I could actually reach out and grab that happiness instead of feeling it slip through my fingers over and over again.

A pivotal moment in my life that allowed me to FINALLY understand my relationship to self occurred in 2018 when I had my second pelvic surgery repair and a partial hysterectomy. I didn't know it at the time, but on the other side of that anesthetic was a whole new life waiting for me that I didn't even know I wanted.

For after this surgery came lifelong physical restrictions, permanent changes I would have to make to my lifestyle and the way I took care of myself and my body to go along with the physical changes, with the most emotional and impactful (although I didn't know it at the time) being the loss of my womb. At the time, all I thought about was being free of pain and I didn't think twice about the

Chapter 1

possibility of any spiritual or emotional attachment that may later resurface with a vengeance down the road, but boy did I find out. Not only was my body no longer capable of doing so many things so as to not risk a third and likely-to-fail surgery to repair any further damage, but I was now missing a vital part of me to which I had unknowingly attached myself and my identity as a woman. This was a very confronting realization for me to process, do some deep healing around, and forgive myself for having essentially "thrown away a piece of my body like garbage" without so much as thanking it for having nurtured, protected, and borne two healthy babies. Instead, my attitude had been more like, "good riddance."

My whole identity as a woman, as a mother to my kids (along with having to come to terms with the fact I could no longer become a mother and carry my child), as a wife, as a healthcare worker, and as a person was rocked and ripped apart to the very foundation of who I'd "thought" I was. My body was changing as my hormones began to have a mind of their own. I was under physical restriction to no longer lift, push, or pull anything over 25 pounds for the rest of my life, and because of this, I was no longer able to perform my job, I was no longer able to do the workouts and activities that I used to do to stay in what I thought of at the time as "being in shape," and I began to experience severe pain and tightness in my pelvis, hips, and legs, which eventually prevented me from walking for more than a couple minutes at a time. I was unraveling at my core, and for the life of me had no idea how to get out of this new nightmare that had become my life. I blamed the surgery for taking my mobility, I blamed the surgery for taking my ability to have children, I blamed the surgery for my body gaining weight as I became more immobile, I blamed the surgery for taking away my decades-long career I had worked so hard for, I blamed the surgery for ripping everything away from me, when in reality that surgery was the catalyst I didn't know I needed to tear down my false belief systems about myself and shove that confronting mirror in my face to take a good long look at the FAKE me that I'd paraded around as.

What was actually being reflected to me were my true feelings toward myself, my inability to show myself love, compassion, and grace, and my inability to forgive myself for being my own bully. I had been breaking my own heart over all those years of self-abuse through toxic inner dialogue, crazy fad diets, grueling workouts, and self-sabotage each time I berated myself for falling off the wagon, skipping a workout, or running through my ever-growing mental list of "fixes" every time I looked in the mirror. I treated myself horribly for decades and honestly had no idea I was doing so because the fake me loved herself, the fake me said these beautiful affirmations and dove into what I thought were self-care and self-love practices without knowing that in actuality, I was externally throwing all of these things at the wall I had built around the fake me persona, but none of them were actually coming from WITHIN, from my heart and Soul that was breaking a little more each day as I continued living my life by showing love, support, compassion, and forgiveness to everyone else, yet always forgetting to, or never even thinking of, throwing a little inward toward myself.

I had to learn to accept that what I used to do and what used to work for my body didn't work anymore. I had to learn that I wasn't the same person anymore. The more I said, "I can't do this," or, "I can't do that," while thinking I was just innocently reiterating the doctor's restrictions for this new me, the more doing so became my new "excuse" for why I was starting to look different. The more my body responded to the story I was telling myself, the more my body answered, "No, you absolutely can't." The more I believed this story, the more my body responded to what I was essentially creating—a whole list of "can'ts" because it was easier for me to justify why I wasn't "in shape" the way I used to be due to something outside of myself, which I blamed for that.

Cue the downward spiral of my deteriorating mental health, self-image, self-esteem, and self-acceptance. I completely fell to pieces just as I had subconsciously asked myself to by denying the truth right in front of me. Instead, I gave in to excuses, fear of judgment, and whispers from the outside world.

Chapter 1

I now know that I NEEDED to experience that shattering of my carefully constructed "self image mask" I had been building my whole life in order to realize that the foundation of myself, the core of what I thought was myself, was still based on the me that I wanted to portray to the world, the me that I thought I had to be to fit everyone else's expectations, the me that I was "supposed" to be —in other words, the FAKE me. And now it was time to let go of the fake me and instead build my relationship to self with a foundation of love, acceptance, and peace within. My task now was to TRULY fall in love with myself, which was something I had never experienced before. I didn't even realize this until I shed that old identity through deep self-reflection, self-forgiveness, and healing. I discovered how I truly FELT, the REAL me, and saw that I had made up a story that I was happy when in fact my internal dialogue was toxic and my Soul was crying. To the outside world I had appeared "put together," but as I dug deeper and connected to myself and my truth, I learned that in reality, the fact was that I had been crumbling inside. It was in this realization that I found my answers, my path to healing, and my freedom through the powerful process of surrender.

I needed to let go of everything I thought I knew and surrender to just being with myself, listening to myself, keeping myself moving forward through all of the tears, anger, and resentment that were being reflected back to me as I proceeded through my hard look in the mirror. If I wanted to change my relationship with myself, and in turn, the way I showed up for myself and my family, friends, and clients, I needed to push forward and continue to surrender and trust. I had to forgive myself for being my own bully.

There is a saying that "until you love what's on the inside, you can't love what's on the outside." Throughout my experience of finding my way back to myself, this deeply rang true. I could do all of the external things and the outside CAN change, yes, but the inside will never stop whispering the truth, the inside will never go away, and the inside has the patience of a saint, so will continue to wait and nudge and speak until you listen. I played that game for decades; I stuffed down that inside voice, turned a blind eye to my truth when I was being shown the façade of the fake me, and fought the good fight until I had no choice but to turn that perseverance inward and fight my way back to myself, where I found true freedom and peace within.

Through consistently showing up for myself, even on the many many days I'd wanted to quit, I processed everything and broke down the false belief system about myself that I'd constructed throughout my life. I recovered myself through trauma healing, past life regression, crystal healing, meditation, a consistent spiritual practice, and the continued love and guidance I channeled from my Angel team. My inner dialogue changed completely; now when I look in the mirror, I no longer twist and turn while ticking off a mental list in my head of all of the improvements I think I need. I now actually SEE myself through the eyes of unconditional love for the first time, and to this day, even writing this chapter, I tear up with a level of self-love I never knew was possible. I am SO grateful to myself for doing this healing, for staying on my journey, and persevering every time I was triggered and wanted to berate myself for still getting pissed off or hurt over it. Instead, because I have literally rewired my brain—including my thoughts, my perspective, my perception of life, and my relationship to self—I can SHOW myself grace and love and gratitude and gentleness as I work through those niggly triggers, which are slowly diminishing.

The shift in my relationship to self occurred in stages. The first was emotional, which encompassed a lot of tears, a lot of anger, a lot of guilt, a lot of resentment, a lot of fear, and a lot of self-actualizing as I peeled back the layers of healing traumatic experiences that held these deep emotions festering inside of them like an infected wound where I could only stuff things down and turn a blind eye for so long until it finally broke open and spread its poison throughout its host. This healing was deep, deep release, which then cleared the way and created the space I needed to replace those deep, heavy emotions with love, peace, and forgiveness. The second stage of my journey was the spiritual aspect of filling those spaces with light

Chapter 1

instead of dark, with love instead of hate, and with power instead of fear. The path of learning how to take radical responsibility for my role in the way my life had been unfolding to that point, learning how to see the lessons and be grateful for them, and learning how to FORGIVE myself for allowing all of it. The last stage was truly embodying self-love for my physical form and it was the final puzzle piece, the last cog that fell into place which opened my eyes wide to the power that I'd truly had within me all along. I'd only needed to look. To pay attention. To give her a chance to speak and to show me the way, and she did exactly that. She showed me the way to love, the way to peace, the way to self-forgiveness, the way to healing chronic pain…the way to FREEDOM.

I have learned that emotional healing is the first step in creating an energetic shift, which then flows through the physical body to heal and repair any symptoms or dis-ease as the shift is integrated lastly into our physical form. I learned that my body was not letting me get away from myself and the unhealed wounds and buried emotions that were wreaking absolute havoc inside my physical form. My body had been speaking to me and I hadn't been listening.
As I build my own dictionary of my body's responses and reactions that show me which things are not in alignment with me, I allow her to teach me, and I allow myself grace and patience as I learn to listen.

The ways in which our Soul speaks to us are miraculous and continue to blow my mind at each twist and turn in this journey while I add to my toolbox of healing practices and modalities I am building as I heal along the way at every stage—emotionally, spiritually, and physically. The mind-body-spirit connection truly has to be in balance and harmony, all together. It took me a while to get this, to realize that as I continue to grow and expand in one area, maybe another area will become out of balance and start speaking to me, but I now know how to listen and fully trust myself to be guided every step of the way in whichever way she chooses to speak to me. The more I focused on myself, the more I was rewarded with positive shifts around me that I had been previously trying to control and uselessly putting all my energy toward instead of feeding my OWN Soul with that energy and listening to what SHE was asking of me.

 "The day I realized that I no longer felt embarrassed or silly placing my hand over my heart and whispering "I love you" was the day I knew deep down to my core that my life had completely transformed."

~Shannon Olsen~

This simple statement of saying and actually MEANING and FEELING the words "I love you" to myself was something I'd chased for YEARS by consuming all the spiritual articles, books, and podcasts at the beginning of my journey that talked about self-love and powerful tools like affirmations for building self-confidence. For years I bombarded myself from the outside with all these things, not knowing at the time that it wasn't from the outside that these words needed to be spoken, but from the INSIDE that they needed to be heard. THAT was the missing piece for me that I'd chased— the next book, the next Facebook post, the next podcast telling me what I needed to do when in reality, it was simply to listen to myself. SHE knew. She ALWAYS knew all along what I needed to do, and she patiently waited for me while I struggled by not truly going within to break the patterns and rewrite the limiting beliefs and stories of who I was and what I was meant to be that I'd been telling myself on a daily basis. Doing that was like throwing flowers and butterflies at a brick wall. These actions were all external, just on the surface, and they were the way I'd lived for decades. External to myself.

As I unraveled and healed trauma after trauma, and slowly picked away at that brick wall I had built around myself, I began to SEE differently, I began to FEEL differently, I began to KNOW differently, and slowly, pinhole by pinhole, I began to let my light shine through that wall. I began to awaken to my own power, my own Divinity, and my own strength and bravery to finally stand in the

Chapter 1

truth of who I was instead of hiding behind the wall of bricks I had so carefully built around me each time I felt diminished, each time I felt scared, each time I felt unsafe, each time I felt unworthy. It was then that I realized the one thing that would now fit between the bricks as they continued to come down, the one thing that weaves its way seamlessly and effortlessly through those pinholes to penetrate deep into my Soul—Love. Unconditional love. The most powerful yet gentle emotion that slips through and transforms everything in its path.

Is this journey over? Have I reached the be-all, end-all of enlightenment? No. Absolutely not. I am still working daily on my embodiment practices, still using my toolbox to deal with triggers, and still uncovering new and deeper traumas to heal. I know I will always continue to do this for the rest of my time on this Earth, and I also know without a shadow of a doubt that I will be OK no matter what. I don't fear the future because I have the one and only thing I will ever need to be my North Star to navigate me through any challenge or bump in the road, and that is ME. I am my biggest cheerleader, my biggest fan, my biggest support system, and when I feel I cannot get to the next step on my own, I am finally OK with asking for help and feel grateful to receive it instead of like a failure for asking for it. I couldn't go back, the same way you can't unsee something or unknow something; it just IS now, and the only direction I head is forward. It is a way of being. MY way of being. The way that I forged for myself by committing to myself and my healing journey so I could reach this state of true peace from within, for which I will be forever grateful.

This seemingly simple realization has completely transformed my life and I solely credit this transformation to one thing—my relationship to self and my connection within. It is why my mission is to share this message, to guide women through their own journey back to self, to light the way to inner peace, to unconditional love, and to monumental freedom through perseverance, healing, and building a strong belief and trust in yourself to find your way as I did. This is my Soul's calling. This is why I am here, and this is why I went through each and every step of my journey in the way that I did, to find myself and come to this exact place where I am meant to be. I have never been more sure of anything in my life, and am beyond excited and blessed to continue on in my mission and purpose as a spiritual trauma coach sparking those beautiful pinholes of Light in your wall, and showing you how to start pouring that unconditional love through them as you too take down that wall brick by brick to shine as you are meant to—in complete freedom and peaceful love from within. Just like rewiring ourselves as we break habits like smoking, nail-biting, binge eating, or addiction, when we begin to see the truth of who we are and then do whatever is in our power to honor that, we begin to think, choose, act, react, and believe differently as we sink into this new way of being. The path is not perfect, no, but it IS created in absolute perfection for you to find and awaken your own power within. The question is—will you choose to follow it?

Be sure to check out the link in my author page for my free guide of simple spiritual practices to begin and strengthen your connection to self!

About the Author
Shannon Olsen

Meet, Spiritual Trauma & Self Transformation Coach, Shannon Olsen.

"Recovering your relationship to self is the greatest gift you will ever give, it's never too late to start, it's never too late to change, and it's never too late to dream" is Shannon's mantra and is the foundation on which she builds her teachings to share with the world.

Meet Shannon, a former healthcare worker turned Spiritual Trauma and Self Transformation Coach, Angel Medium, Advanced Crystal Master, Reiki Practitioner, and founder of her spiritual wellness business Vibrations of Light.

Published as a co-author in two best-selling books, Shannon shares how she began her spiritual and Soul led entrepreneurial journey to create true happiness and peace from within, and makes it her mission to guide other women to trust and believe in themselves to do the same while letting go of false beliefs that keep them stuck in the cycle of people-pleasing, putting themselves last, and self-sabotage. Shannon's dream is to have women awaken their Divine spark within and recognize how incredibly powerful and needed their unique, authentic self is in this world.

Connect with Shannon and join her growing community here: https://linktr.ee/vibrationsoflight444

Chapter 2

Living Our Ancestors Wildest Dreams

Jacquie Fenske

The amazing life I lead today would undoubtedly exceed the wildest dreams of my ancestors. I would venture to say that many people today could make a similar claim if their lives were viewed from their ancestors' perspective. Yet we say our lives are ordinary, that we are ordinary people taking advantage of what comes our way. However, the truth is, we hold the power to either grasp opportunities or allow them to slip through our fingers; the choice is ours to make. We can not only fulfill the most ambitious dreams of our grandparents but also realize our own aspirations. How fortunate we are to live in this era, where we have the ability to transform these dreams into reality.

 "Anything you can do, or dream you can do, begin it: boldness has genius, power and magic in it."

~JW von Gothe~

What are you and I doing to make the most of life? To start I challenge you to answer these three questions along with me.

Who am I?

What do I want?

What is my purpose?

Who am I? I am complicated. I have at least two personalities and I'm okay with that. There is the very public Jacquie and the very private me. Very few people truly know the private Jacquie. That's my protection. And that protection allows me to escape my current reality by withdrawing into my private persona when necessary. I'm not about to give that hidden space away too readily. Maybe that will be in my tell-all memoir when I reach the age of 102. Until then only a few are welcome to know that side of me. I have a bubbly, happy personality and a pensive soul. I'm bold but shy. I am impetuous in love but decisive when decisions need to be made. I love being around people, but I'd rather be alone. I'm dedicated to growth. But I know self-sabotage all too well. I'm just trying to find my way through life. And the path I take defines who I am.

I love my life today. Maybe it's just because I've reached a certain age and all the normal life experiences that form my history allow me to now be in this moment. There hasn't been a eureka moment or a traumatic incident that I can pinpoint as the catalyst for a significant life transition. There isn't one monumental event that defines who I am. Maybe it was there, and I didn't let it define me. I mean how many people get elected to political office? Yes, getting elected to a political office changed what I did for a while, but the earth didn't tremble under my feet and the skies didn't open to make me think of myself differently. I've got baggage but never felt a need to change dramatically to still be able to live my best life. Change has been a gradual process. Over the years I've acquired knowledge that, had I possessed it earlier, might have led me down a very different path. Yet it's my attitude more than my victories or losses, that truly defines me. I absolutely love life. I make my choices.

Chapter 2

Sometimes they aren't the best choices and sometimes I must regroup, refocus, and move on. But I own my choices.

I've consciously surrounded myself with remarkable individuals who inspire me to strive for improvement, nurture my creativity, and achieve more. I want the world to share my excitement for the opportunities and experiences that life offers us all. Finding ways to inspire others to embrace life has become my mission. Of course, not everyone wants to choose to embrace life. Pity.

If you were to ask 12-year-old Jacquie what she would be when she grew up, she would have confidently said, "Teacher, lawyer, and spy." It's quite something to look back from this experienced stage in life to see just what Jacquie's done with her first memorable "intention." The story of how it unfolded and continues to evolve is a tale for another time and place. And growing up? Well, growing up is overrated.

Perhaps, someday, I might convince myself that I've truly grown up, but it's unlikely to happen tomorrow and certainly not today. Until then I will look at life with the naivety and trust of a child.

I've come to understand that to live your best life, you need to embrace a childlike mindset—remain inquisitive and receptive to new ideas. It means being open to what the universe hands to us. Even with my vivid imagination I could not have dreamt of the opportunities that came my way. I've been blessed but I've also been willing to say yes. It's all too easy to talk ourselves out of taking action, often driven by self-doubt, fear of risking our reputation, concerns about what friends might think, worries about financial instability, and the ever-present temptation of procrastination. We often tell ourselves, *Maybe later,* or *Another time would be better.* BS.

Lesson One: Just do it. Say yes!

 "Only those who risk going too far can possibly find out how far one can go."

~ T.S.Eliot~

Choose to say yes to opportunity. You know it's for you if you can't get the damn idea out of your head. If you don't make the move someone else is going to claim your opportunity. I have started writing a book many times over. My goal was to leave behind a legacy of inspiration and encouragement for my kids, to give them a head start in living their best lives. But shiny objects caught my attention, distracted me and took me in other directions. My book was written but written by Elizabeth Gilbert. When I read *Big Magic*, I found myself predicting the next page before even turning it. If only I hadn't procrastinated, I could already be on a book tour. I could have answered the *Who am I?* question by adding *author* to the list. Yet, I prioritized other matters or found excuses, and now, years later, I'm finally on the path that will allow me to add *published author* to my identity.

In my mind I've never been good enough. This has been one of my excuses. Why I feel that way even to this day is for a therapy session. I was an honours student most of my school life but only a "just honours," never a solid 90% in any subject. I never had a lead role in any drama production. I was never the one school boards looked to to lead committees and I don't think it evenly remotely occurred to any of the three premiers I served with to appoint me to a ministerial position. While I chaired some impressive committees, I never held the title of Honourable Minister. I could still fall back at any time on the excuse of not being able, ready, or good enough to keep me from pursuing some of the opportunities that have come my way. That's still how I feel. That is self-sabotage.

Yet, somewhere along the journey of life, that feeling has transformed into the very thing that propels me forward. No eureka moment, just a sad feeling I've tried to cover up by pushing those

Chapter 2

thoughts aside. I need to prove to myself more than anyone else that I can be good enough and not just good enough to be a seat warmer but good enough to make a difference. That insecurity has become one of my biggest motivators. Choosing to bury that feeling beneath a flurry of activities has resulted in my ability to make a substantial impact on the lives of individuals, my community, and my province.

I've got a lengthy list of feel-good moments. And I'm willing to bet that if you take a moment to reflect, you'll find an amazing list of "feel goods" in your own life. Just think, what if I had allowed my fears to prevent me from stepping up? What if I had hesitated to put my name on an election sign out of fear of losing? I've gained so much more by stepping forward than I ever would have by stepping back.

Who I am is a reflection of the roles I currently occupy and the responsibilities that come with them. I was a politician and a teacher, but those terms no longer define me. I am a mother, a wife, a daughter, an entrepreneur, a community connector, an ideas person, and an influencer. That will continue to change as I choose to say yes to future opportunities. And that's not just okay, that's great.

Lesson Two: Use your talents or lose them.

I believe we are on this earth to move beyond ourselves. When we neglect our talents, choose to ignore them instead of nurturing and developing them, we not only do a disservice to ourselves but also to the world around us. Can you build? Can you speak passionately and convincingly? Can you sing? How often have you heard of people with singing talents that stop singing only to lose their ability? Can you learn new things? Most of us could keep learning. I've challenged myself to learn new skills to help me get over election losses. One of those learning challenges I set for myself was mixology. I've never indulged in many cocktails because after two drinks I'm done for the night, so I didn't know what was in a Brown Cow or a Cosmopolitan or anything beyond orange juice and vodka, let alone the technique used to mix those drinks. Taking a mixology course after one election loss became my diversion. I may have gotten the lowest mark in the class, but I did pass and have the certificate to prove it. After another loss at the age of 60, I learned to ride a motorcycle. It's a good thing I've won more elections than I've lost, or I would amaze you with all my newfound abilities. That and it would be hard to find the time to keep up my skill levels. I think my motorcycle riding skills are falling prey to the adage, "use them or lose them."

Lesson Three: Take action.

This is the lesson that yields significant results while requiring only small steps to attain your desired outcome. To begin, ask yourself, *What do I truly want?* Set your intentions. I'm still working on getting better at this. I need to take time to be specific in my vision. When I am specific in what I want it's amazing how easily I end up getting exactly what I've envisioned. This even extends to something as seemingly mundane as envisioning available parking spaces when I'm running late for a delivery. Give it a try. If you see the finished result and work back from there to identify the steps, you will find step one might be as simple as telling someone your idea or making a phone call.

When directing a play, we directors set opening night as the end of our timeline, and then work to build the production from that point backward. We plot out all our key deadlines; costumes, sets and rehearsal schedules are all set to ensure that we are ready when the curtain rises. But it all starts with a single small action. It starts by selecting a script and booking the theatre for the production. What does that take? Perhaps a phone call. Perhaps an email. And then things just keep rolling out.

One scorching June day as Mom, Dad, and I gathered around their kitchen table, daydreams of owning an ice cream shop filled the air. (And did I mention just how hot it was?) I had brought home some milkshakes and casually expressed how wonderful it would be to have our very own ice cream shop. To my surprise, they revealed

Chapter 2

that they had been discussing the very same idea the previous week. Dad had a craving for an old-fashioned milkshake made without fillers, just ice cream, cream, and flavor.

That afternoon, we brainstormed, created a menu, and chose the name, Fifendekel. However, the crucial turning point was taking action—right then and there. We picked up the phone, dialed McKay's Ice Cream in Cochrane, and set up an appointment with Mr. McKay for a few weeks later. I believe that had we not moved beyond mere discussions and taken that step to schedule the meeting, our dream might have withered away.

Fast forward over 40 years, and we are still savoring the sweet results of that phone call, which led to that pivotal meeting. It's the same phone call that brought McKay's Ice Cream to Edmonton in 1983, shaping our journey into what it is today: a successful pie shop cafe.

I have a dream, not as lofty as Martin Luther King's but one I think might one day be extremely important to preserving the unique aspects of rural life and in creating dynamic and thriving communities. In politics, one is acutely aware of the numbers game. Throughout my political career, my primary focus has been on amplifying the voices and addressing the needs of rural Alberta. The decisions made around legislation and policy are too often made to address the needs of big city populations and in doing so can negatively affect rural lifestyles. While not always intentional, these decisions can result in unintended consequences for rural regions.

As the countryside depopulates and major urban centers grow, I've come to realize the importance of urban residents championing rural causes. Hence, the concept of Experience Alberta was born—a company aimed at creating and supporting experiences, events, and businesses in rural areas, with a strong emphasis on urban participation. Remarkably, the name was available at corporate registries, and that was the starting point of an exciting journey. We stand on the verge of some remarkable agritourism experiences.

So, if I were asked today *What do I want?*, my answer would be that I want to be an integral part of building rural tourism in Western Canada and the expert people go to to seek advice from in that area. I aspire to achieve the financial stability, which would enable me to become a benefactor in growing tourism opportunities. Have I mentioned I love my life? It's going to get even better.

Lesson Four: Build your network.

We can't possibly do everything we dream of on our own; at least I can't. Help is needed. Working with others not only eases the burden but also makes the journey more enjoyable. As the saying goes, "It's not just what you know, it's who you know." Besides driving my desire to promote rural life, the other benefit of having been involved in politics is the network of contacts I have built. To continue building my network, I attend events, utilize social media and volunteer. I think that if you threw an Alberta issue at me and needed some advice if there wasn't someone in my network that could help you there would be someone in the network who would have the contact you need. From finding an eye doctor on the weekend to treat a family member to putting a friend in contact with an international buyer for their product, my network has always come through. Of course, one shouldn't leave a network unattended. People move and life passes, so your network needs ongoing nurturing and building. This takes some effort, whether through making a phone call, sending an email, or, even better, attending a face-to-face meeting.

Franks on the Farm is a little event that started as a thank-you to volunteers of one of my political campaigns, however it has stuck around and morphed into a casual rural networking experience. Gathering over hot dogs around an open fire, people from various backgrounds come to the farm to rekindle old connections, establish new ones, and enjoy the beauty of the rural landscape. Every Monday morning, five of my inspirational contacts meet via Zoom for just thirty minutes to touch base, identify opportunities and support each other's dreams. It doesn't take much and it's so good for the soul. Solitary confinement is one of the harshest punish-

Chapter 2

ments you can give a person. We are human beings, and we need human contact. That's what the network can provide. Our networks serve as invaluable tools and support systems, enhancing our personal and professional lives in countless ways.

The last of the three questions to answer is *What is your purpose?*

As one's life situation changes, so too does one's purpose. When I was young, I wanted to fall in love. I wanted to be the centre of someone's universe. I was so insecure that I didn't see myself as the centre of my own. Over the years my family has become the centre and at other times my job has. It's taken a long time for me to feel valuable enough to become the centre of my own universe. Silly as it seems it's my reality. When I make a list of my accomplishments, I see that I've accomplished a great deal over my lifetime, but that list is full of items that were created to meet the expectations of others.

I remember when I turned 40 thinking I was done meeting others' expectations. Age would be my excuse for any silly thing I did that made people think less of me.

However, that year I ventured into politics, pressure to meet others' expectations seemed to grow rather than diminish. Now, as I approach the age of 70, I'm considering using this milestone as a new reason not to conform to others' wishes. It'll be an interesting experiment, and I'm eager to see how it unfolds.

I envision becoming that vibrant, eccentric woman with a distinctive fashion sense who draws people in with irresistible charm and inspires them to make the most of their time on this planet. Let's see where this journey takes me.

I've never explicitly considered my mom my role model, but I've come to realize that she has been my enduring inspiration all along. Selflessly dedicating herself to others, my mom has consistently embraced new roles and exceeded expectations. She made the bold decision to leave behind city life and the comforts of running water and electricity to live on a farm in the same house as her mother-in-law. Upon arriving at the farm, she even had to learn how to drive.

Jacquie Fenske

In the course of her life, she mastered the art of milking cows, tended to a thriving garden, and raised five children, complete with all the challenges that come with parenting. Then, in her mid-50s, alongside my father, she embarked on a new business venture in an industry laden with red tape and narrow profit margins. This business has not only provided decades of opportunities but has also created cherished memories for family and friends. Through it all, she has been the glue that held everything together.

My mom is a remarkable woman who completed grade 10 at the age of 13, showcased her talents as a singer on the radio, and fearlessly ventured into entrepreneurship. She's undoubtedly the real risk-taker in our family. She recently advised me to ease up on work, fearing that I might end up like her. However, at the age of 90, although she has slowed down a bit since her recent hospital stay, she remains active by continuing to tend her garden and is still willing to serve pie at the restaurant.

When I reflect on her life and her unwavering dedication, I can't imagine why I would want to turn out like anyone else but her. My purpose is clear: to strive to be as great a leader and role model to others as she has been to me.

One day I want to share the stories of my wonderful life experiences with you in hopes they will inspire you to find joy in life. I hope my journey and my lessons will encourage you to take the risks you are dreaming of to make them more than dreams, to make your ideas real. The four lessons have served me well. They are my gift to you on your life journey. It is a wonderful journey. Enjoy it. Define your purpose now knowing it will change over time. Hopefully your transition will be as gradual and rewarding as mine continues to be and you will become a leader that exceeds your ancestors wildest dreams.

 "If your actions can inspire others to dream more, learn more, do more, and become more you are a leader."

~John Quincy Adams~

About the Author
Jacquie Fenske

Jacquie Fenske is a living example of the reward that comes from taking risks and pursuing one's passions—a life many dream of living.

Originally trained as a teacher, she taught junior and senior high school, and did a unique teaching stint teaching at the Drumheller Penitentiary. Her dedication to community service led her to serve on Strathcona County Council and as a Member of the Alberta Legislature. She also played a crucial role as the Acting Leader of the Alberta Party.

Jacquie is always involved in community organizations and has chaired several local and provincial boards.

Driven by her passion for connecting with people and promoting Alberta, Jacquie has co-founded two businesses that promote people, events and communities throughout the province.

She understands and has been involved in every aspect of business through her role as a managing partner of her family's 40-year-old Edmonton business.

Jacquie firmly believes in making a difference through action, not just words. Her dedication to action-driven results sets her apart as a true woman of impact.

www.jacquiefenske.com

Chapter 3

How I Transformed My Body From An Enemy To An Ally

Becca Kyle

Sunlight bathed the canyon walls in a brilliant, warm glow as the glorious reds and oranges of the rock structures lit up like fire. I let out a contented sigh and then slowly breathed in the beauty that surrounded me as I gazed upon the sweaty yet joyful faces of my family. Experiencing the beauty of nature with loved ones is something that reconnects me to them and God, and fills my soul. I couldn't take for granted that not only was my body well enough for that nine-mile hike, but I was able to experience it with the people I love the most. Exploring the beauty of this world with others is a true gift, and for me, exponentially compounds the glory of nature's bounty. To once again feel the capacity to do so was such a positive shift for me toward the life that I'd dreamed of.

Why was a simple hike such a life-altering moment for me? The days that I'd struggled simply to take a ten-minute walk in my neighborhood weren't that far behind me. I had experienced long periods when my nervous system and anxious body would beg for a walk, but I'd have to will myself to put one foot in front of the other and fight through the debilitating fatigue and pain I lived with daily. For years my normal life was filled with chronic symptoms that made it extremely difficult for me to function and get through each day, much less thrive.

Many times I sat on my living room floor feeling like an utter failure. I felt that I had failed my husband, my kids, my parents, my clients, and my friends. It was like my brain was trying to think through thick mud, and impending doom was the most common emotion I felt. Sometimes the unexplained pain and fatigue made it difficult for me to even tuck my kids into bed. I had massive dreams and goals for my life but the path to achieving them felt filled with booby traps and health-related roadblocks. I felt overwhelmed, hopeless, and incredibly frustrated. My body felt like an enemy that I had to fight daily but I had no battle plan, no weapons, and nowhere to hide.

I was no stranger to chronic illness, as my health first started to tank when I was three years old. I ran chronic low-grade fevers and dealt with unexplained fatigue. If I missed a night of sleep, I got sick, so my mom hesitated to allow me to attend slumber parties when I was a child. I was a good host for infections and missed weeks of school fighting Epstein Barr virus, cytomegalovirus, candida, and strep, which was momentarily a mystery, but was finally found in my nose. As a child, I was tested for everything from lupus to leukemia, and my mom never got definitive answers to my chronic issues.

As an adult, for decades I flip-flopped back and forth between feeling okay to miserable. In 2006, I was first diagnosed with adrenal dysfunction after I had overexerted myself. I'd completed graduate school in a year while working twenty hours a week, then hiked to the bottom of the Grand Canyon to camp in the July heat where the temperature was 130 degrees at the bottom. Enduring those days of extreme heat and exertion during that trip left me unbelievably depleted. I felt like I had been hit by a truck, and the deep, intense fatigue debilitated me. Sunlight and music became intolerable to my nervous system, and I grieved these losses immensely. It took six solid weeks of intensive intervention with strategic supplements, purposeful midday rest, and stress reduction to start to come back to life and for my energy levels to improve.

Chapter 3

The first time I felt like I could listen to music again was when I knew I was improving.

I spent the next decade trying to function as best as I could through ups and downs, fertility issues, traumatic and difficult births, and postpartum seasons. It wasn't all bad, as I had some seasons of feeling pretty good! I tried to make the most of my life in between symptom flares, in part through faith and part through a fierce determination to live the life I wanted to live. I gave all I had to my family and job, and tried to surround myself with people who loved and supported me no matter what. There were also times I felt I could have won an Academy Award for pretending to feel fine, which led me to sometimes feel like I had an invisible illness. If I looked fine and acted fine, people became quite confused if I sometimes confided to them that I actually felt terrible.

I had to put my health first, which isn't easy to do with three young children. I learned that I wasn't a cup or a pitcher to pour myself out of to serve to those I love. Being in an exhausted, overwhelmed, and depleted state, I couldn't be the mom, wife, friend, daughter, or sister that I wanted to be. I had to retrain my nervous system to be a bowl, and it became my job to fill up my bowl with self-care tasks like rest and play activities. The purpose of these activities was to delight me and bring joy, restoration, and peace to my life. I also made myself get out of hermit mode and schedule time with friends and loved ones.

These activities became some of the biggest keys to my long-term wellness. I had to get back to the basics of health and wellness and realize that so much of what I needed was free or cost very little! Sunlight, grounding, community, spending quality time with friends and family, walking in nature, dry brushing, sweating, using castor oil packs, humming, gargling, and taking Epsom salt baths became my weekly rituals. I also had to learn how to ask for and accept help.

As a young girl, my favorite phrase was, "I'll do it mine own self." At some point, I'd made the unconscious decision that needing help was a bad thing, and if I needed help, it meant I wasn't enough.

What I had to learn is that there is power in being vulnerable and that needing help simply means that I am human. It took practice for me to be able to accept help and I had to get out of my comfort zone to find the support I desperately needed. My husband sometimes had to force me to sit and relax while he made dinner and it was extremely hard for me not to go into the kitchen to help.

What about serving those I love? Well, I fill up my bowl and serve them from the overflow. I realized that I have to take care of myself first, and that doing so isn't selfish at all, it is, instead, the most selfless act of service for my family. The burnt-out, strung-out, exhausted, and overwhelmed version of me didn't have the capacity for patience, fun, life lessons, and adventures, however , the peaceful, energetic, focused, and joyful version of me did. So, I had a choice to make. Which version of me did I want to feed? Which version of me would give me the life of my dreams?

Around this time, I found the wellness support I didn't even know I needed and fell in love with functional health. A three-month migraine had taken me down, and it wasn't my family doctor or my neurologist who found its root cause. It was a dear friend and Functional Nutritionist who helped me figure out that I had extreme histamine issues that were driving my migraines, anxiety, and insomnia. This was the same practitioner who'd previously introduced me to the world of health and wellness genetics and taught me how to support and honor my genetic blueprint. With her guidance, I had gotten pregnant with my rainbow baby after experiencing a previous miscarriage at eight weeks. This experience sparked a massive passion in me to share this type of care with the world. I wanted to add purpose to my experiences with pain, and I knew that helping others as my friend had helped me would allow me to do that, so I went back to school and received a Functional Diagnostic Nutrition Certification.

I began to feel better as I actively worked on engineering my daily life to win with rest, play, nutrition, nature, fellowship and reducing inflammation, but even with all the effort I put toward improving my physical health, I still avoided dealing with the emotional grief

Chapter 3

I'd kept buried for so long. I had hit rock bottom after my third pregnancy and most traumatic birth, during which I'd experienced placenta accreta, a life-threatening condition. The postpartum depression that followed triggered a massive decline in my mental and physical health. My nervous system and adrenal function struggled under the weight of emotions I had shoved down for decades.

I knew I needed to come back to who I still was, who I had always been, and who I longed to be, but that I needed help to do so. Even though I had become certified to use functional labs to support wellness and I could support my gut health, hormones, and inflammation all day long, I knew I needed more. If I were to truly heal, I would have to release the grief, trauma, and pain that I'd buried deep within myself for years.

To be able to truly approach my wellness in a way that would allow me to address multiple root causes, I couldn't hide any longer from this hardest and most important work, and needed strategic support to do it. So how exactly did I transform from feeling like my body was my biggest enemy that was holding me back and preventing me from living the life I desired to deeply understanding how to bring my body back into ally territory to thrive? It wasn't simple, and the process required work, but it was 100% worth it.

Eradicating infections, balancing my hormones, and biohacking my lifestyle was easy compared to feeling my feelings. I'd kept most of my emotions locked up tightly, except for frustration, anger, bitterness, and rage. I could quickly access those feelings, which had caused my relationships to suffer, and I didn't know how to start dealing with this.

There are moments in life when a pivotal experience or person can change everything. For me, that person was Holistic Pelvic Care Provider Miriam Bouve, who taught me that nothing that stays hidden ever heals. I decided to work with her to heal the birth trauma I'd never processed, but had no idea just how much our work together would help me in so many other ways. I learned how unprocessed emotions, stress, and trauma live in the body, causing medical conditions, general anxiety, depression, and decreased vitality for life. I will shout to the rooftops for the rest of my life that she saved me. She showed me how to allow the emotions to reveal themselves to me, honor their truth, then finally release them.

At the beginning of our first session, I was nervous and didn't think much would happen. Miriam was so patient with me as she instructed me in breathwork and explained that while I may laugh or cry or be surprised by an upwelling of emotion, to just go with it and let it be what it needed to be. I started focusing on my breath and the soothing music she played and at first, nothing happened. Then out of nowhere, I began to sob and wail. The noises that erupted from my mouth sounded like a wounded wild animal. For the first time in my adult life, I released the pain and grief I had shoved down to survive.

I booked a three-month program with Miriam and over time, experienced such a lightening of the mental load I had carried for so long. The final theme of our work together was to fully reconnect me back to my body with love, grace, and forgiveness. I explained to her how frustrated I was with my body, that I felt like it was holding me back from going after my big juicy goals, and that it had failed me. Miriam helped me realize that my body hadn't failed me, and it wasn't out to get me. She empowered me to talk to myself gently and compassionately, make peace with my challenges, and show my body unconditional love exactly as it was. Little did I know at the time that this was preparing me to discover not long after that session the root cause of my lifelong chronic health issues.

I made incredible progress in my health but still experienced symptom flares that were triggered by high stress, and knew I was still missing an important piece to my health puzzle. I could feel fine, then get hit with a multi-week symptom flare out of the blue. I ended up discovering my answer while supporting a client who was also missing a puzzle piece. I suggested that she fill out a questionnaire that would tell us the likelihood that she had tickborne illness and coinfections. Since I was experiencing a symptom flare at the time, I decided to fill out the form myself, just so I could check it off

Chapter 3

my list. After I tallied up my results, I was floored; I had almost triple the number of points that correlate with tickborne illness. I knew I needed to test. I recalled having pulled ticks off myself as a kid while I nervously awaited my results. What I discovered changed the trajectory of my life.

First, I cried. Tears of frustration, and relief poured down my face. I had my answer, but it also potentially meant a lifetime of managing a chronic condition. I'd tested positive for Borrelia and Bartonella infections, which are bacteria that are common in tickborne illness and coinfections. Then I took a deep breath and smiled. I chose to be empowered by this information instead of allowing it to make me feel like a victim. I finally connected a lifetime of unexplained health dots, and for the first time, my life of health issues made sense.

As I already had a background in functional health, I set about interviewing multiple specialists in the tickborne infection and immune health space. I compiled this information into a two-year protocol to address all of the variables needed to clear my body of these stealth infections so I could go into remission. There is nothing more empowering than going from feeling like a medical mystery to being seen, heard, and validated for the first time in decades by others in the health field. I had found my missing puzzle piece.

I continue to find incredible healing with Miriam, who supported my releasing old trauma, grief, and limiting beliefs. I had to let go of stuck negative emotions to make space for peace and joy. The great unlearning began so I could discover who I was, what I wanted, and what I was capable of. We humans simply aren't meant to bear our burdens alone. God designed us for fellowship, community, and love. It was in the telling of my story and truly being heard that I finally started to crawl out of the emotional black hole that I had been in since the birth of my last child.

I know what it's like to be an exhausted, irritable, overweight, and anxious insomniac who feels like she is failing herself, her family, and her business. I also now know what it's like to move toward my vision of ideal health, feel joy and contentment for no reason, get restorative sleep, have abundant energy, and feel confident in my body. I did what it took to become a wife, mom, friend, and business owner who is now fully present with an increased capacity to live a fiercely vibrant, connected, and fulfilling life.

But when I began writing this chapter, my body started to flare again for reasons I didn't understand. Even though I had made an incredible amount of improvement, I had a nagging suspicion that something in my environment was triggering symptom flares again. I went into super sleuth mode and although there were no obvious signs of mold in my home, I knew the symptom presentation well enough from working extensively with clients suffering with mold toxicity to hire a mold remediation expert to assess both of my attic HVAC units. Sure enough, both were covered in toxic mold. The old me would have been devastated by this. The new me says, "Challenge accepted." I'm now going to hit the ground running with remediation and a mold detox with full faith and hope that I will get better.

Here's the deal: we humans want to victoriously reach and forever remain at the top of our health mountain, but that's not how life works! Sometimes through no fault of our own, we are exposed to things that make us sick and we must drop back down into a valley and heal again. So, I will show up for myself over and over as often as I need to and do what I need to do to live the life of my dreams.

If you are experiencing a season of more health valleys than mountain tops, know that you aren't alone. Your body is capable of healing and coming back into balance. You are powerfully and wonderfully made. Find a practitioner who sees, hears, and believes you and will fully support your wellness journey. Show up for yourself every day the best way you can. Some days that may simply look like getting out of bed, brushing your teeth, and going back to bed, and that's okay. Take one step at a time up the mountainside. As James Clear says, "Get 1% better every day," and you will get there. Your body is not the enemy, it is your biggest ally, and I encourage you to show it unconditional love, grace, and compassion exactly as it is right now.

Chapter 3

My mission is to make the world a better place by improving health, one person at a time. Without my history of health issues, I would have never discovered my true calling. In the end, these experiences shaped me into the practitioner I am now, and became a gift in my life that taught me patience, resilience, and compassion. My passion is helping others to not suffer for years as I did by utilizing tools like functional labs to find true healing opportunities in the body, which gives me a deep sense of purpose.

When I had to decide how I wanted to show up for myself and the world, my business coach tasked me with writing my "billboard statement," which is: *I want to be an inspiring, badass changemaker, empowering, passionate, and fun, and I ask myself in everything I do, "Will this help me change the world?"* I asked myself this question before committing to writing this chapter and if just one person reads this and doesn't feel alone in his or her health journey, then it was worth it. May God bless you and keep you.

About the Author
Becca Kyle

Becca Kyle is a resilient and accomplished Certified Functional Diagnostic Nutrition Practitioner who is dedicated to guiding individuals on their journey to optimal health. Her deep passion for understanding the intricate links between nutrition, lifestyle, and well-being has positioned her as a trusted expert in the field. Becca's personal health odyssey showcases the transformative power of determination and resilience. Overcoming her own battles with tick-borne illness, chronic fatigue, IBS, and anxiety, she not only restored her well-being but became a beacon of inspiration for others.

With a unique blend of empathy and scientific insight, Becca collaborates closely with clients to uncover the underlying causes of their health challenges. By using advanced wellness tools and personalized protocols, she empowers clients to regain their health and vitality. Becca's expertise has earned her features on various podcasts such as The Health Detective, Kick Unhealthy Relationships to the Curb, and The Birth Junkie.

When she's not supporting her clients, Becca loves to read historical fiction and spend time with her husband and three boys hiking, swimming, and seeking grand adventures.

Connect with Becca

Visit my website: https://holisticobsession.com/
Find me on Instagram: @myholisticobsession
Find me on Facebook: https://www.facebook.com/holisticobsession
Join my free Facebook Group: Preventing Burnout With Holistic Health Strategies

Chapter 4

A New Lens of Authenticity

Michelle Seguin

Do you live authentically? Do you know what living authentically means? I thought I did, but I really had no idea until I was forced to learn.

Like most of us, I traveled through life the typical way, having a family and a career. While at work, I strived to do the best possible job I could. At home, I gave everything I had to ensure that my family was taken care of. I attended all my kids' hockey and football games, was there for them when they needed help with homework, and ensured there was always food on the table for supper. To me, living authentically meant making sure I had the best possible life based on what I thought life should look like.

Then one day, my life completely shattered. It wasn't until that moment that I came to realize I had lived my whole life unauthentically in one way or another. I had not intended to live this way, but because I experienced a traumatic childhood, at a very tender age, I created a facade based on the person I thought I "should" be. I believed that anything I felt inside didn't matter.

Over the years, I became very good at molding myself to be what everyone else wanted me to be. I put away any parts of myself that I felt did not fit into any of my many identities by placing them in a box within myself. No one was ever allowed to see those traits as I was the only one that knew they existed.

Then came the day I was no longer able to hide behind those many identities I had created, so I had to start really digging into them to discover what was authentic to me and what was not. I started by exploring my "work" versus my "home" identities.

The Financial Controller

The first identity I looked at was my identity at work. As a financial controller, I had an idea of what I thought a professional was supposed to look like, so I conformed to present myself as that. Some of the qualities I exuded included having a strong work ethic, high integrity, being detail oriented, trustworthy, reliable, confident, efficient, and very structured. While at work, I never showed my personal feelings; my business decisions always came first.

My mindset was that no matter how big the job, I could put my head down and get it done to the best of my abilities. I never allowed myself to joke around and I showed little to no empathy when it came to business decisions. As a child, I had created the belief that emotions showed weakness, and therefore being "professional" meant showing little to no empathy.

Setting clear boundaries was also an issue for me, as I always believed that I needed to give more of myself to show my worth to the organization. While I was at work, I always put the company's needs before my wellbeing. I went to work sick. I went to work when I had pneumonia. I worked from bed when my doctor put me on bed rest due to a fibromyalgia flare-up because the company expected it. I lived and breathed what the company needed over what I needed for me.

The Mother and Wife

The second identity that was a major factor in my life was my identity at home. As a wife and mother, I had high integrity and morals, was trustworthy, reliable, very empathetic, and loving. At home, I

Chapter 4

loved to ride Harley Davidson motorbikes and do burnouts. I was very laid back and comfortable going wherever the wind blew me. I did not care for excessive structure or organization, and always chose what was in the best interests of my family.

While at home, I was happy as long as my family was happy. But I always chose to take on all the stress of my kids and husband as my own. I never took personal time, and my happiness depended on theirs. If one of my kids called to say they were maybe going to stop out at our acreage, I canceled all my plans because I might get to see them - even if only for a few minutes.

A few traits showed up in both my personal and business identities but for the most part, I never allowed them to cross over. In fact, I used to make comments about how I was two different people; one person at home and someone completely different at work.

At that time, I was proud to be divided. I had created a belief system that if I was to show traits of my authentic self at work - such as empathy, compassion, or the fact that I was a Harley-riding rebel - I would be judged. I truly believed that showing some of those authentic traits would affect my career and people would think I was not the right fit for holding such a high-demand position. At work, I made multi-million-dollar decisions and never blinked an eye. Yet at home, I sometimes struggled to decide what to make for supper.

Back then, the version of myself I was at home was definitely more aligned with my authentic self than the version I showed people at work. I always felt uncomfortable at work because I never allowed any of my vulnerable traits to shine.

On the other hand, I came to realize that I had not been fully authentic at home either, as I never put myself first. I never allowed my full strength and confidence to shine. If I chose to take care of work requirements and was not there every moment for my children or husband, then I felt like I was letting them down. However, if I chose to go to a football game and therefore wasn't at work to fulfill a need for the business, I felt like I was letting the company down. Even though I balanced them as best as I could, I always put everyone else's needs ahead of my own, and whether I realized it or not at the time, this added intense stress to my body and soul.

The Shattering of Identities

For many years I lived with these huge differences in identities until my oldest son passed away in 2013 after a short illness. This threw everything into turmoil. I felt like I lost all of my identities at that moment. I could no longer go to work and be the same person I used to be, as I was grieving so intensely that it was hard not to show emotion at work. It became impossible for me to not show my feelings and who I truly was. But this caused me to worry even more that my job would be affected. I felt like I was breaking the cardinal rule of not showing emotions at work and worried that I would be seen as weak and fragile.

My identity at home completely shattered as well. I was no longer "just a mom," but also a mom who had lost a child. My life felt completely broken, and the stability I had felt with my little family of four was completely taken away by his passing. Through my grief, I tried to figure out what our family would look like now. No matter how much I gave of myself to my other son and husband, I could no longer fix them and make things better. At home I had been "the fixer," and I felt I was losing that identity as well.

Losing my son was the most difficult thing I will ever experience in this lifetime. You can go through life thinking you know who you are and what you stand for, but in the blink of an eye, it can all be stripped away. In no longer knowing in the slightest who I was anymore, I did the next best thing I could think of—I chose to lean into my work identity more.

I had no idea who I was any more outside of work, so I became determined to take the next steps in my career to become a CFO. I now see that I did this in order to escape my grief and create a new identity for myself, anything that would help me define myself in clearer terms. But all that decision did was make me feel even less

Chapter 4

like my true authentic self. Both at home and work, I slowly faded away and became someone I was not.

Trying to be a grieving mother, a mother to my other son, a grandmother, a wife, and a business woman was a stress I constantly put myself through. I was not just burning the candle at both ends, I was burning the whole candle all at once.

Eventually, all the identities I had been trying to create and make work all came crashing in as my body started shutting down. I had a full-on fibromyalgia episode which would normally last a week or so, but this time, I spent close to two years on bedrest. My health continued to deteriorate and I no longer had any idea who I was or what I wanted from life any more.

All of my identities were stripped away from me at that time; the only one that remained was the "sick Michelle" identity I had also carried with me for many years. This was a difficult and horrible time in my life, but I was in such constant pain that I had little time to focus on who I was or who I wanted to be. Everyone around me was treating me like a frail, fragile flower that was put on a shelf to look at. This was incredibly traumatizing, as I no longer felt heard or seen. After some time, I eventually realized that this experience was the universe telling me it was time for me to figure out who I was at a soul level once and for all.

The Fake Reality

As my health finally started to change for the better, I had to face all aspects of my life head on. After close to two years, I was ready to heal and find my true authentic self, no matter what it took. I was tired of trying to make my authentic self be what everyone else expected, and it was time to find out who I truly was for myself.

One of the first things I realized was that the two main identities I had created and lived for many years of my life were both FAKE. In reality, I was neither identity, and I had never been true to the person who mattered the most - ME! I came to realize that I was truly betraying myself in both worlds.

It always felt so uncomfortable when living my work identity because that was not the person I was. I had some of those traits - such as being strong and confident - but I presented myself in a way that was very unauthentic to the person I truly am. Some of the ways I was unauthentic to myself included being unempathetic, non-emotional, and showing little compassion.

Then when at home, I also had some of those traits, but I allowed childhood traumas to cloud what I thought that identity should look like as well. At home, I presented myself as less independent and less confident than I was. I showed more emotion, but I also buried a lot of deep emotion within my body.

I realized that the stress my body was feeling from conforming to these varying identities was causing me even more stress, which was fueling my fibromyalgia and chronic pain. Somehow, I had allowed my authentic self to be completely taken away at both work and home. I chose to put everyone - my kids, husband, boss, coworkers, and even the company - ahead of what I needed for me.

The Awakening

Unfortunately, it took the tragic loss of my son for me to start putting myself first. Whether I realized it or not, I started to acknowledge my needs by grieving how I needed to grieve, and doing what I needed to do for me to start moving forward in my life. The problem was, I still wasn't listening to my body or my soul, so the universe tried one last Hail Mary and put me on bed rest to give me one final opportunity to learn how to listen to my soul.

As I started to figure this out, I became shocked. Throughout my life, I had always prided myself on behaving like a different person than who I truly was, and now I came to realize that in having done that, I had been separating myself further and further from my soul. I was totally forgetting who Michelle was, and how special she was. I had to take ownership of my lack of authenticity, which was hard to face.

Chapter 4

It was not the company's fault that I'd felt like I had to be someone I wasn't while at work, and it wasn't my family's fault that I'd never spoken up for things I may have wanted at home. I was so busy being my interpretation of what everyone else wanted me to be that I did not even consider my needs or who I truly was. On top of this, I had allowed my childhood trauma to completely silence the adult version of me, just like the child version of me had been silenced.

I had allowed my job to take away my true identity as I fit the different molds I had created. Then motherhood and being a wife required a different identity. All these instances caused me to create new versions of myself that weren't authentic at all. And it took tragedy for me to realize I was ready to live authentically in this one life I had been given.

At first, accepting the realization that I had created all these versions of myself was extremely difficult. I really did not want to take off my rose-colored glasses and see everything for what it was rather than what I had made it seem for so many years. However, after losing my son and my health, I realized the rose-colored glasses had already been removed - they were no longer shielding me from anything. So I became ready to look at my life and myself through a new lens of authenticity. I chose to prioritize myself and truly, honestly look at all aspects of my life through a clear lens. I also had to choose to take full ownership for where I was and how I got there.

As I started to move forward - one step at a time - I worked through each part of those identities and determined who I truly was, what was authentic to me, and what was not. I had to examine each trait I had exuded in those identities and determine if it was something I had created or if it was truly authentic to me. To follow my path to authenticity, I had to learn how to listen to my body and not ignore the signs it was providing me.

One of the first things I had to accept was that I felt so out of alignment with who I was within my accounting career that I chose not to go back into the industry. Some may ask if this decision is permanent or temporary.

I don't have that answer yet. At this time, I still have no desire to go back to it, and in the event that I ever do choose to go back to a career like that, the most important thing will be for me to ensure that I continue being fully authentic. For now, I choose to not go back to it, as I see how truly unauthentic I had been while doing that work, and I do not want to live like that ever again. If, at some point, I do decide to go back to that career and I notice old habits returning, then I will address them immediately and, first and foremost, stay true to myself.

As far as my identity at home, I have chosen to merge some of the traits from my work identity that were authentic to me as part of my true identity. What I learned from intense grief and tragedy is that at the end of the day, authenticity is all we have. I will never separate myself into two different people again, no matter what.

I am choosing to pick the authentic parts out of each identity and merge them into the true authentic version of me - the person I know I am. I have also had to integrate new things into this new identity, such as setting boundaries in my life. I am now very clear that I am my priority in life, and that as long as I am happy and healthy and take care of myself, I will be able to assist others. I also have learned that it is not my responsibility to take the stresses of others (especially my children and grandchildren) onto myself. This allows them to take on their own stresses in life to learn and grow from, and also allows me to live a much more peaceful life with little to no stress.

The authentic version of Michelle is strong, confident, independent, loving, empathetic, compassionate, and most of all, the version who has an unwavering love for herself. She knows that she needs to be truly authentic in all ways, and puts herself first knowing that she can be a much better mother, grandmother, wife, and business woman when she does so. She has learned to trust herself and her decisions, and knows that as long as she follows her strengths, she is unstoppable.

Chapter 4

Unfortunately, it took intense grief for me to find my authentic self. Losing my son was the hardest thing I will ever go through in life, but through this intensity, I have found myself. Rather than living life behind a facade, I continue to choose to live from my soul (authentic self) and I revel in the amazingness of every day. I listen to my body when it speaks because it is telling me something for a reason. As long as I follow my soul's nudges, I will never be wrong, because I am now living from a space of true authenticity, and no one knows better what I need in life than my soul.

About the Author
Michelle Seguin

Michelle Seguin is a best selling author, Radical Recovery of Self Coach and Heal Your Life Teacher and Coach who specializes in helping adults and teens find their true authentic self. Guiding her clients through a process of self-discovery and healing, she supports them in finding peace and fulfillment by creating a strong connection between their mind and body.

Michelle understands that a person can create different identities depending on the people they are around and the environment they are in. Through her experiences with this, Michelle has developed a clear understanding of how the limitations and identities we place on ourselves affect our emotional and physical health, and subsequently opened her heart and soul to the power of helping others.

Michelle's open and loving heart helps her clients feel safe while she works with them to find their personal power and feel confident in everything they do. Michelle gently supports her clients by giving them the tools they need to release the chains that hold them back.

You can find Michelle at:
Website: www.peacefulconnections.ca
Facebook: www.facebook.com/peacefulconnections
Email: mseguin@peacefulconnections.ca

Chapter 5

Notes From Beyond

Nichole Walczak

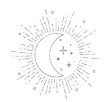

With a heavy heart she looked up at her oldest brother and could see the pain and anguish in his eyes. She knew there was nothing she could say or do to help, as she was also feeling the exact same emotions as him. It was almost 10pm and the hospice was quiet with only the sound of a light wind through the open window. She could hear their father's breathing becoming more and more shallow as they both sat on either side of his bed. Six seconds would go by, and a breath, then eight seconds, followed by another shallow breath as the time between breaths became longer and longer. Her thoughts flooded her mind with memories of her big strong dad pushing her on the swings, bike riding, swimming. She felt an agonizing, sharp pain in her heart. She looked up at her father's face, not realizing that it would be for the very last time. His yellow eyes stared past her into nothing. *What is he seeing right now? What is he thinking? Can he even hear us?* She knew she would never get those answers. She tried to focus on his breathing again but only heard silence. She knew then that he was gone. He had taken his last breath.

That was my experience with death. And as many people who have experienced death it was the hardest thing to endure. Death is always perceived with such dark and solemn tones—grey, black and bleak. I am not here to bring up that pain. I am here to share with you my experiences of death and how looking for signs from the other side can allow you to find your spiritual awakening and even save your life.

I want to help guide you into opening your eyes, heart, and mind to what is out there. Maybe I can even change the way you perceive death, just as my dad and a few others did for me.

Why are soo many people afraid to talk about death? Why, when you start talking about it, do people often change the subject because it's "too negative" or makes them feel "uncomfortable"? I have always been fascinated with the thought of death. I listen to true crime podcasts, follow a pathologist and a hospice nurse on Instagram, and have always enjoyed walking through cemeteries. I find their calm and quietness help ease my worries. Most people find them creepy and haunting. I have even told my best friend which song to play at my funeral: River Jordan by Michael Jackson. I have been called morbid many times but the truth is that I just don't see death as most people do. I see it as a birth, a beginning instead of an ending, something to even be excited for. I know I sound completely backward or even harsh. I know the stabbing feeling in your heart when you think you may never see a loved one again, never hear their voice. It's torture. But what if their death was them returning to their original home? What if you KNEW that when a loved one passed, they were finally at complete peace, happy, and being their true selves? If that person got to tell you that they were now enlightened and free, wouldn't you be happy for them? Would it help to heal your shattered heart?

Imagine if after people died, they left notes saying, "I am no longer in pain. I am the happiest I have ever felt in my life and will continue to be with you and guide you until we meet again." Would we still look at death through a dark lens? Or would we see it in a new form, like a metamorphosis of the human body? Well this did happen to me. And it didn't happen just once either.

Chapter 5

My dad was diagnosed with stage IV Pancreatic Cancer. This was a complete shock to all of us. It wasn't until he started losing weight that we became concerned. On the advice of a friend, he finally went to the Emergency Room, where he waited eight long hours. Thinking back now and reading his texts, I have a few regrets. I wish I had called and talked to him on the phone while he waited; he was never much of a talker though. That is one of the hard parts of death, the "what ifs" or the "I should haves." Those thoughts can drive a person crazy with regret. I try not to dwell on those. He was given three months to live. I remember hearing that and thinking, *Wow, he will be gone by September.* Imagine being told you only had three months to live. No more chances, nothing will help. It all seemed soo unfair: My dad died ten weeks after we got the diagnosis. That's all we had with him. I took time off work and that was the best decision I ever made. Listen here! Work will ALWAYS be there. Even if you get fired there's OTHER WORK. You ARE JUST A NUMBER. They will replace you in minutes. DO NOT LIVE TO WORK! WORK TO LIVE! Your family is what should come first, always. I spent almost every single day after his diagnosis with my dad. It was soul wrenching watching my strong dad suffer and melt away into nothing. I thought to myself every day, *What kind of God would let someone suffer like this?* I had absolutely zero faith. I felt betrayed. I was angry. My dad was only 61 years old. He had four grandchildren under four years old. Life is not fair. Fuck cancer. Those were my daily thoughts. I fell into a dark depression. I was angry at the world.

The day came when he finally got to die. I say that because he suffered for so long that death seemed like a blessing. I was playing some music quietly when ironically Stairway to Heaven by Led Zeppelin started. It was the last song my dad heard. He loved Led Zeppelin when we were growing up. "Mike, Dad is gone," I spoke to my brother. We both looked at each other in silence. I kissed my dad on the forehead and told him I loved him and said thank you for everything. Time seemed to stand still. This was the end. Then, suddenly in a matter of seconds, I felt a surge of energy go through me. All of my hairs stood on end. The feeling took my breath away.

And I smiled! I was suppressing an urge to laugh. In the saddest moment of my life, why was I feeling this way? I felt so enlightened. Then at that exact moment my brother asked me, "Nikki, do you feel like Dad is here?" That was exactly what I was feeling. He took the words right out of my mouth! I told him with a big smile, "Yes!! I do!! He's here Mike, he's here and he's smiling! And he's soo happy and he's soo light!" I had always felt such a heavy presence around my dad when he was near the end. My brother then said through his now happy tears, "I feel like he's hugging me! He's putting his arm around my shoulders," and I just nodded and agreed, saying, "He's here and he's free!" We both soaked up that moment for what felt like a blessed eternity. The whole room was surging with an energy, and with it was the feeling of peace. After a few moments Mike quietly asked me, "Nikki, do you still feel Dad here?" I didn't. We both knew he was THEN truly gone. That moment will be with me forever. I know that was his spirit leaving his heavy and strained shell of a body. I can't explain and I didn't see it, but I just knew in my heart that he was smiling and happy. He had left me my "note" that he was okay and would be with me always.

Before my dad went into the hospice, I asked him if he believed in such things as reincarnation. He just shrugged. So I asked him if he was to come back as an animal to give me a sign which animal it would be. Once again, as a man of few words, he just smiled and finally said, "I'll come back as a skunk." That night driving out of the hospice parking lot a few hours after his death, what did I see but a big skunk scurrying away. I smiled. Thanks Dad.

The first time I received a "note" from someone who had passed I was twelve years old. My friend Helen called me one night around 9pm, crying hysterically. Her dad had just taken his life. I went over to her house. My heart ached for my friend while I tried to comfort her. She told me through her tears that her dad was in Hell. Her faith taught her that when someone died by suicide, their souls go to Hell. But this idea felt completely wrong to me. I am not a religious person and I believe everyone is welcome to their own beliefs

Chapter 5

however, that just seemed wrong. I felt it in my heart that he was not in Hell, that he was okay. I thought to myself, *I wish there was a way to show her that he's okay, to help her see!* Then I got an urge to turn on her radio. I hesitated for a second thinking it would be intrusive, but that urge just got stronger. I walked across her room and turned it on. I immediately recognized the song that was playing. It was by my favourite artist Shania Twain. The song was It Only Hurts When I'm Breathing. I turned to my friend and shouted, "Helen!!! It's your dad! He is not in Hell! He's okay! Listen!!'

The lyrics of that song talk about finally moving on, being over the worst, and being free again. I have heard that song a million times and never once considered it to be about suicide. At that moment, with my friend, that song was made for her.

The song rang to me like bells going off! The lines in the lyrics were telling her he was free again. I knew that her dad was giving her a "note." It was his way of telling her that he was alright. We are still friends to this day and she told me that it helped bring her some peace. I truly hope it did. Because I know with every fibre of my body, it was him.

Sometimes we will see signs that may not even be from people who have passed, signs that help us through the most challenging moments of our lives. We don't know who they're from, we just need to be open to receive them. If you think, *Oh, that's just a coincidence*, those signs will just pass you by. I am glad I didn't let one of these signs pass me by as one sign helped save my life. The year was 2019, and my son had just been born a few months previously. I hadn't known then, but I was suffering from severe Postpartum Depression. My thoughts were dark. I didn't feel the joy or happiness that comes with a new baby. I felt regret and loss for my life before. I felt that my husband and my son would be better off without me. I started to plan how to end my life. I never told a soul. It was a dark secret between myself and my depression. I even knew which bridge I was going to use. I chose this specific bridge because it is a long way down to the river below. One night as I was driving toward that bridge I thought, *Just one sharp turn of this wheel. It will look like an accident. No one will know. I can't continue, I'm not good enough.* Those dark thoughts had overtaken me. I felt my hands turn to rubber and took a deep breath, ready to turn the wheel. Suddenly from the corner of my eye I saw a massive white owl swoop down right beside my car and glide along with me as if it was trying to stop me. I quickly turned my wheel in the other direction and continued straight, then pulled over. Adrenaline surged through me and tears fell down my face as I got out of my car. I looked up to see the owl perched on the light post above me, looking down. I knew in my heart it was someone protecting me, watching me. I made a promise out loud to myself and the owl that I will never allow myself to get that close to the edge again. I could only imagine what I looked like standing in -30° celsius weather, crying and talking to an owl. I told myself that I would seek help. I did, and I won!

I am a huge advocate for women and even men who are suffering from Postpartum Depression. I have experienced it firsthand and know the detrimental impact it can have on your life. I want more people to feel safe to talk to someone if they are feeling the same way. Anyone. You are not alone. You are not a bad mother/father if you do not feel a bond with your baby right away. You do not have to feel bad if you have dark thoughts. Get help. Do not isolate yourself. I can now openly talk about my experience with PPD. I am thankful every day that I didn't give up. I wouldn't be here today if it wasn't for my husband. During the survival time of the newborn stage, he was always the one who got up in the night, did most of the diaper changes, cleaned my pump parts, and even the house. I opened up to him and felt safe confiding in him with how I was truly feeling. He is and always will be my rock. We have two amazing and happy toddlers who keep us on our toes and I am thankful every day that I listened to the sign I was given. I will keep my promise to that owl for my family and for myself.

I had my daughter in 2020. During the pandemic, the world seemed to be shut down. I was on maternity leave and never felt more alone. I met a neighbour who turned out to become one of my best friends. She was unable to work and for months, came over every

Chapter 5

day. She helped me with my two babies. She cleaned and made food. We "worked out," if you can call it that. She even changed poopy diapers! We became two kindred spirits. Little had I known that she'd needed me just as much as I needed her. Christmas time came and I helped her decorate her tree. The previous years, she had been too depressed to decorate, as her dad had passed suddenly near Christmas in 2017, so Christmas always brought up memories of her dad. I grabbed one ornament out of the bin and held it up, admiring it. She said, "That one has some of my dad's ashes in it!" I very carefully handed it to her (I did not want to drop it!). She held it in her hands, looking at it. At that moment I felt a strange feeling overcome me. I was almost too embarrassed to say this out loud but I am glad I did. I said, "Mandy, your dad is here! He's here right now, I can feel him, he's happy you are decorating your tree, he wants you to know that!" Then suddenly, out of nowhere, there was a loud knocking sound. We both looked up and right outside of her window was a woodpecker pecking at the siding. It seemed as if it was watching us. We both laughed and smiled. She told me that woodpeckers always reminded her of her dad. She cried remembering him. I smiled and silently thanked her dad for dropping a "note" to say hi to his little girl.

When a loved one passes away, they will always send us signs. It may not be right away, but they will reach out to you and continue reaching out as long as you are open to receiving the signs. I am wearing my butterfly necklace in my author photo. I bought it the week I found out my dad was ill. I wanted something that reminded me of being a little girl again—butterflies. That same day, my brother Ryan sent me a photo of a blue and yellow Swallowtail butterfly that had died. It was a little depressing, as I compared that butterfly to my dad. I didn't think anything of it until a week before his funeral when I was in Las Vegas and saw a massive butterfly in the air. It was the exact same species of butterfly that my brother had sent previously. I pointed to it and it fluttered down and landed right on my finger. It stayed there not wanting to leave. I walked around for a bit, took a few photos, and knew it was my dad once again, giving me a sign that all is okay.

Nichole Walczak

I am at the beginning of my journey of receiving notes and can't wait to see where it takes me. If you are in a state of grief and feel you will never heal, open your eyes to the beauty around you.

Do not let the darkness of death overshadow the light of your life. Allow the energies to come to you and know, there is more after death. There are notes to be found everywhere. Look, and you will find yours.

About the Author
Nichole Walczak

Born and raised in Calgary, Alberta, Nichole works at a Children's Hospital and a Supermax prison, and is also pursuing her hobby of voice over. Being a mother changed Nichole in incredible ways after she overcame the struggles of Postpartum Depression (PPD) with thoughts of suicide. Now happy with two bouncy toddlers, Nichole enjoys helping those struggling with the pressures of parenthood and bringing awareness to the serious struggles of PPD.

Witnessing her father's death was the moment Nichole experienced the miraculous transformation of his spirit leaving his body. Although it was heartbreaking, it was also the most enlightening and empowering feeling Nichole had ever felt. She knew right then that her father was truly gone from his suffering body, and had been freed into the spirit world.

Nichole wants to reassure anyone who may have lost someone or is afraid of losing someone that there is indeed something more after our spirit leaves this world, and encourage them to never give up because they too may experience their spiritual awakening!

You can find Nichole at:
Instagram: http://www.Instagram/Nikki_Walsky
Facebook: https://www.facebook.com/nikki.walczak.161/

Chapter 6

Positive Mind, Positive Vibes

Kimberly Stefiuk

What does being a positive mindset person mean to me? And where will it lead me?

The Cambridge Dictionary defines *positive* as, "full of hope and confidence, or giving cause for hope and confidence, a positive attitude." I'm at a point in my life currently that I am still growing on my path to knowing the true meaning positivity and how influential one's perspective is on things. My main mission in life for the last few years has been learning how to forgive so I can grow in love for myself, and most importantly for my family. The evolution of who I was, to where I am now is something I am so proud of, and I want to share my story as it creates space to talk about the impact of TRULY believing in yourself.

So here we go, I AM this person, this is HOW I work, these are MY deepest beliefs about MYSELF and an explanation if you will, of who I am. To those that know me personally reading this chapter I want to first acknowledge you and hope you can sit in my energy and words without judgment.

Born in the Yukon until age 3, and then growing up in small farming community, I was taught to be kind, be helpful, build people up and not break them down, say nice things, say thank you, play, and explore. I only have fond and loving memories of my childhood. I am proud and so thankful for having the kind-hearted, loving, and very generous parents that I had growing up, who let us grow up without any expectations to be anyone but good people, and even more important, good to Mother Nature, especially animals. I understand and am so grateful for my advantage to having been raised the way I did experiencing the things I did and did not.

My mom specifically taught me to be kind to people, even the ones that don't deserve it. She taught me to include everyone, and that making comments/judgements about other people is rude and not to do it, and don't stare! As a little girl I remember watching my mom among the people in our community. I saw a beautiful woman who always showed up with love first and believed in seeing good things in people and situations. She instilled in me so many powerful beliefs about life and what a good person does. I'm forever thankful for the mom that I got, and hope she knows what an impactful and loving person she is. She spreads love and light to all those around her and her legacy continues through me as I raise three perfect children with her support.

My dad taught me the meaning of the saying, *If you don't have anything nice to say, don't say nothing at all.* Maybe that's why he is so quiet. Good man. He showed me what hard work means, as he mined gold and copper around the world. And though due to a typical working-away schedule he missed a few moments, none went without him fully there in spirit. I knew his love was always with us and I am so honored to tell him how much I appreciate every single second of his hard work during my childhood. He has been retired for over six years, but I don't think he's slowed down that much. He is either a fisherman in Slave Lake, a farmer's helping hand, "Lenny Poppins" (babysitter for my kids and/or nephews), or my personal arborist/animal sitter/carpenter/gardener/recycler, etc. He knows what it means to do what you love. He does whatever he does with complete love and respect and is always willing to help

Chapter 6

when he can. I'm so thankful he's my dad, and his legacy lives on in my children as I see them exhibit his kindness and care with all animals.

After high school and until I became a mom, numerous times I felt my higher self connecting with me, and I felt a deep understanding of who I was, even though my ego told me what I was experiencing wasn't true. I always just knew that opportunities that I allowed or denied were exactly meant for me. There is no way I would have known how to explain it to anyone back then, but now I know that all that happens, happens FOR, and by me. I asked my supervisor/mentor at work if he thought I was weird for letting go of things as easily as I do, for not sitting in sad/dark emotions for long, for being able to see the good in a bad situation. Thank goodness he said no, and even made me see my ability to do so as a superpower, which I know it is! Not long after I began to see myself as a powerful person, I was (not by chance) given an opportunity to really discover myself in a deep and spiritual program called the Hoffman process. After a week-long retreat, I was allowed back into my life, but as an awakened and refreshed version of myself. It was suddenly so clear on who I was: a spiritual being living in a physical world. Some transitions happened very quickly for me not long after this retreat: a relationship that felt like nothing could ever come between us shattered, lifelong friendships disappeared, a new me emerged, I knew exactly what I wanted, and I trusted the process to lead me where I am meant to be.

Throughout my life whenever I was asked the question or given feedback from a coach/teacher/or supervisor of who I am, or what my strengths are, I usually said words like, "kind, positive, caring, calm, fun, loving," and now I see *those* are the words that define me, that quite literally created my path and led me to exactly where I am meant to be, here. I *am* all those words. I am enough the way I am. But for about seven years, I was in a vulnerable and sacred time of my journey, becoming the new version of me, not just Kim anymore, now a mom and wife. The expectations that were put on me from sources that offer love and support became overwhelming and undesirable. I was a woman who loved and wanted peace first, and who believed the best in any situation, but I found myself feeling the need to defend who I was, as how I was raised was looked down on. I felt like who I was, wasn't enough, like I wasn't worthy of the life I had or that the things I could offer my children weren't valuable. I was in a constant race to get ahead of any possible outcome to look like the "perfect mom." I felt as though some looked at me as if they could do better, and I began to believe it too. I was in a dark and ugly place for a while, and I felt the rumble of need for change within me. During lockdown, I was given the space to shut out the world and not have to explain anything to anyone about what my family was doing. In the time we had together, we spent hours and hours exploring the nature around us on our quarter of land. We found old farm equipment hidden in the bushes and went on little hikes in the back and made forts amongst the trees. That time created moments for me to connect with my higher self in Mother Nature's presence. I will always treasure that time, as it allowed me the space to fully step into myself. And my kids were witnessing my transformation.

Having sped through so many milestones both good and "bad" that led me to this keyboard to type my story, I take pride in it all, even the really icky situations. I send love to those moments, as they made me who I am today. The journey from then to now seems so long ago, but it involved many emotionally charged events which I took full responsibility for creating and recreating over again until I finally learned my lesson, and then I experienced my second and most powerful spiritual awakening. One cold winter night, I didn't feel like the "real me." I just kept feeling the urgency to get out of the chaos and out of all the things to do. Go outside and clean our holiday trailer. I had turned negative over the years of allowing negative energies to wash over me. I had changed and honestly hated myself. I hated how I talked to my husband, how I was always angry and felt no patience, and like I was doing the worst job as a mother. I felt like I had failed, and it was a dark feeling. In the trailer that night I found a old journal from about 10 years earlier, inside the journal was a letter I wrote to myself "I trust and allow my

Chapter 6

higher self to lead me to where I am meant to go" Those words were an affirmation to me that even though things felt like the worst they could get, I was MEANT to be here, and I was MEANT to go through all that. I was ready to start over again, and holding on to feelings of anger, or to victim type energy would not hold me down any longer. I am enough exactly the way I am, and I no longer let a single person's ideas of what I am have any impact on me. My kids deserve a different kind of experience, one of light, care, peace, acceptance, and unconditional love.

Leaving the trailer, I felt a huge pull to reconnect to Source as quickly as I could. I first googled guided meditations and then felt instantly better just slowing my mind. This led me to slowly reconnecting with past mentors and friends who shared this same spiritual awareness, including joining Shannon's new spiritual sister group, where I knew I would be accepted. No matter what energy you are in, you can match and even magnify it by reading like-minded messages and interacting with others who feel similarly. My soul craved positive, loving energy so badly that I felt instantly fulfilled once I started looking for it. It was a choice I had to make, and it took me many years to come to terms that there was no finger pointing anymore—I had always had my power, and I had made the choice to shut up and not be me.

The first message I received from my higher self was that I *needed* to forgive, which involved a lot of work to figure out what or who I should be forgiving. After hours of reflecting and journaling, maintaining a strict morning routine of walking the dogs and being in Mother Nature for some quiet time, learning AND practicing how to properly communicate the hard stuff with my husband, I finally felt the urge to let go of all the hurt and really stay in the moment. Writing my chapter for this book was really an amazing experience, as I really had time and space to dig up some covered-up emotions and as always, everything worked out as it needed to so that I received the right support to get the process done. Learning to forgive is something I honestly had a hard time believing I would ever see the "other side" of, but my journey is mine and everything is mine to perceive and receive. We can only do our best with what we know. I have a sticker on my vision board that reads, *If you can't forgive, then you need to reflect*. I reflect by journaling, which allows me to release frustration and anger, as those emotions don't belong in anyone's system. Anger and low-energy emotions only build more anger and low-energy circumstances in the physical world. Loving and positive emotions create more loving and positive circumstances in the physical world. It's simple: Be love, get love. Hard situations are now like opportunities for me to grow, be better, and let love flow.

Making the choice to be a positive person is 100% about perspective and staying committed to who that future version of yourself is that you want to become. I committed to a new habit of making daily lists of what made me happy until it was no longer a habit, it just was. My list includes things like doing a morning routine to take care of myself first before anyone/anything else this includes hygiene, vitamins, stretching, taking time daily to be around animals and take care of them lovingly, surrounding myself around positive energy, and removing negative conversations and situations from my kids' proximity. I hated the amount of time I found myself mad and frustrated—it's not a fun place to be. The first achievement I reached was literally remembering to put on my face cream every day. I had never prioritized myself before. Spending time every day and night to do something as simple as applying face cream feels like I am a well cared for queen. I compliment myself by telling myself things like, "Hey good looking!" or, "Wow you're looking glowing today!" I feel important and loved when I talk to myself like that. No one but me quit loving me first and no one but me will ever stop loving me everyday as much as I now do. Loving yourself the most and taking care of yourself as best you can lead to a beautiful life. Being a parent and having the opportunity to spread the love on to my three children is my biggest job here on earth, I've committed to taking back my power and making the changes that need to be made.

Chapter 6

I could tell I was on the right track of becoming my future self one very typical morning while getting the kids ready for school as their energy was all over the place. Old Kim who had been stuck in anger and impatience would have probably scolded them and left the house annoyed, but instead I felt calm, and all the right words came out of my mouth. I felt so good that it became easy to do and is still something I'm trying to master! I was finally starting to see proof that I was aligned with a positive path. I went to the bathroom, looked at myself in the mirror, gave my reflection a high five, and told myself that I was proud of myself for showing up as this positive loving version of myself.

When I trained my mind to include statements like, *I am kind, I am calm, I am patient, I am love and light and I live in love and light,* and then act in alignment with those statements, I am kind to myself and those around me, I show patience for myself and others, and I approach all situations with love and light. If I feel a situation does not align with me, I create more space for more of *I am* statements, and it helps me to stay connected in where I am aiming to go.

There are infinite ways to look at a situation, only you get to choose the energy you receive from it. I choose to spend it looking it from love always, I am always looking for the positives. Show me the positives!! We only have the moment that we have in our hands, moment by moment, day by day. Slowly with practice we all are capable of anything, it's only up to us to decide how we are showing up. WE create our future by how we are moment by moment. Reflect and forgive. Reflect and forgive. Where are you showing up in lack of where you wish to be? That's where you start. I lacked peace in my life, so I created it. And I worked hard and am happy where I am on my path of wellness. I'm working at everyday to improve myself in some way always. From 5am workouts, to every day for over year listening to positive mindset podcasts, there is so much more I need to grow but I trust that I know the way. Who you are spills over into your life all around you, be who you want to be.

About the Author
Kimberly Stefiuk

Kimberly Stefiuk is a 37-year-old mother of three residing on a farm with her husband Neil and their farm-raised dog Meatro (short for Meatball). Surrounded by a diverse range of horses, from team roping horses to minis, their home thrives on love and strong coffee. Kimberly's journey is centered on how she learnt to fully trust in her higher self to lead her where she is meant to be, which led to self love and forgiveness for herself first. Through thirteen years of spiritual practice, she has learned the power of maintaining a positive perspective, setting herself free time and again. As an Educational Assistant, Kimberly shares her uplifting energy, knowing that love is the highest frequency we can reach. Working in early childhood education, she believes that every interaction contributes to making the world a little more loving . Kimberly Stefiuk is a beacon of love and positivity in her family, community, and beyond.

Chapter 7

The Soul Speaks to Us Through Our Bodies: How Listening to My Body and Self-Nurturing Led Me to Trust My Voice and Own My Power

Jennifer A. Telford

I clearly remember the moment as a young woman in my 20s when I felt a piercing pain in my left breast. I was in my kitchen and looked at my boyfriend, who was standing across the room. A haunting feeling took over as my heart said, "You are not the one." Hearing this whisper frightened me, as I didn't want to believe I could be feeling this. Nor did I even know if what I was feeling was true or real. My heart was feeling one thing, but my actions spoke another.

I kept silent, unable to express what was coming up. Externally I was there, but internally I was yearning to be elsewhere. I did not want to hurt my boyfriend, and I was afraid of losing my comfortable existence. Up until then, he and I had been inseparable.

I didn't fully comprehend where these feelings were coming from and why I would feel them. Was I harboring a lie? The happiness of being in love had shifted and I was experiencing a strange and lonely inner dialogue that would start me on a path of healing, and I could feel my breast pain getting louder and louder. Was my heart whispering to me through my breast? What was I afraid to gain if I actually honored the voice? What was I afraid to lose if I continued to live in denial of my voice?

Little did I know that this would become the beginning of a long journey in learning to love myself through the mirror of my relationships and finding that through loving myself, I could reverse a health issue before it became serious.

Two years passed without me fully speaking my truth, going through the motions, acting as if I was still the same girl he had fallen in love with, while this pain in my breast persisted. At this point I shared with him a bit of what was on my heart, but still did not take any action to leave. I was afraid of what this would present in my life. When you have built a life that revolves around the belief that you and this person will be together forever, anything that threatens that becomes something to ignore.

I recognized that I was seeing signs of verbal and emotional abuse. I will never know the reason for his part in it. I want to share how it made me feel and how I healed. I felt small, I felt that my voice was inadequate. At times he spoke critically to me around friends, finding fault with my words. I felt embarrassed. I felt like a mouse and I shut down. I felt like a shadow of my former self as my inner light was diminishing.

As a result, I made some choices as a way of avoiding truly dealing with what I was hearing in my heart and experiencing in the relationship. My coping choices came from a place of not yet being in my personal power, as I lacked belief in my worth.

I became more aware that lifestyle factors influence our health and different aspects of our lives, such as emotions and experiences. In her audio cassette, *Breast Health*, Christiane Northrup, MD, says, "Our every thought we think, the culture in which we are living, the food in which we eat, the atmosphere and the colors that we are around and the lighting all affects our breasts." I began to under-

Chapter 7

stand how this external stressor, and how I was feeling about it inside, could be correlated to my breast pain.

I focused my energy on healing the breast pain. The one thing I could feel good about was caring for my body. Since my body sent the first sign of communication within me, loving my body felt like the right place to start my healing process by beginning to connect with these feelings.

Self-Care and Self-Love were unfamiliar concepts to me. They weren't part of any language I spoke, but they became what I began to do to heal this imbalance. My Self-Care included learning about herbs to support my breast health and using them as external oils, as some herbs have specific nutrients beneficial for breast tissue. I realized there weren't any products that I knew of for women to love, honor and acknowledge their breasts. Inspired, I created a product to encourage women to give love and care to their breast area and provide a proactive and empowering way for women to take personal breast care into their own hands. The product I created is called Breast Caress Body Oil.

Creating the breast oil was like healing generations of women who had been disconnected from their own self nurturing. When we do not fill our own cups, it can cause resentment or exhaustion. Embracing my breast health became a symbol of nurturing my own value and worth and empowering others to do the same. Self-care and Self-Love were now giving me a voice and purpose.

In sharing my process of starting to heal my breast pain, The FIRST step in my healing was connecting with my body by tuning into its sensations and honoring what my breast needed.

I reflected on the qualities of what I was feeling in the breast: denseness, throbbing, persistent, piercing, stinging, and constant are some of the words that best described my breast pain. I allowed myself to tune into these sensations and listen.

To support my body, I began doing self-breast massage as loving and embracing my body through this became an expression of the love and care I gave myself. Self-breast massage was a way for me to positively affect the breast tissue by stimulating lymph flow to release toxins. I was naturally called to do this, like a divine download. Self-breast massage became a beautiful self-care ritual, complementing the oil I created.

Allowing myself to tune into what I was feeling in my body enabled me to listen to the messages that were being whispered, enhancing trust in my intuition. By trusting my intuition, I was learning to trust myself.

Connecting with my body revealed an even deeper emotional dialogue in my heart that sounded like self-negating beliefs. These self-negating beliefs were saying, "I am not good enough." Whose voice was that? Knowing now that at an early age we can formulate beliefs that are not about our true divine self, I can only think that my father not being fully present when I grew up created that belief, and that my inner beliefs at an unconscious level were attracting a partner who made me feel that I was not good enough and my voice was inadequate.

It is important as women for us to recognize how our inner beliefs from our unconscious childhood wounds may energetically contribute to attracting unhealthy relationship choices. The wound becomes stored energy in your body, thus creating a stuck emotional pattern that contributes to stress and manifests as physical symptoms. The messages that our body sends through dis-ease may be surfacing matters of the heart.

In my continued exploration of understanding this correlation, I referred back to Christiane Northrup, MD. In her audio cassette, *Breast Health*, she references the book *The Creation of Health*, by authors Carolyn Myss and Norman Shealy M.D., which discusses how the breast relates to the fourth chakra, which is the heart chakra, and notes several examples of fourth-chakra issues, like holding on to past hurts or resentments, relationship addiction (why a woman stays in a relationship that doesn't support her), emotionally unfulfilling or abusive relationships, being emotionally unavailable, not feeling worthy of being loved, and doing something or being with someone when your heart is not there.

This was my second validation, which gave me a deeper understanding of why I was experiencing this breast pain.

This led to the SECOND step in my healing, which was that I responded to my emotional dialogue with love and compassion to process these emotions.

Recognizing that an emotional dialogue and inner beliefs were surfacing was difficult, as they were telling me things that were hard for me to confront and that I couldn't believe were coming from me. By responding to my emotions with love and compassion, I became more important to me and able to start releasing the emotions that were keeping me stuck and creating dis-ease.

1. First, I recognized that there was an emotional issue that needed my attention.
2. Next, I stepped into what I was feeling and acknowledged these emotions, even if I did not understand them or was in denial.
3. I set my intention to resolve situations that needed healing. This meant forgiving myself and my relationship with a family member, loving myself more by loving the inner child in me that was calling for my attention, and responding to my situation in a different way.
4. I created a vision of the desired state I saw for myself and took a step back to see if it matched my current situation.
5. I journeyed into wellness through journaling, affirmations, wellness coaching, deep relaxation, regular exercise, good dietary habits, meditation, bodywork, energy healing, and other heart centered practices.

The THIRD step in my healing was implementing new lifestyle changes.

This required me to commit to creating new habits for myself and staying accountable. Doing my self-breast massage, using herbal oils, seeking support from health professionals, checking in with my emotional health, and continuing my Journey into Wellness helped me make the necessary shifts in my health, and I continued adding things over the following years.

Sharing this three-step process of self-nurturing that I was intuitively guided through not only started healing my breast pain, but taught me to nurture a deeper relationship with myself, which strengthened my attitude and belief that I am worthy and have value, which inspired my self-confidence. I became able to reframe my self-negating belief by voicing and feeling that I am good enough.

My courage began evolving: the courage to let go and make needed changes for myself. I went from fearing my voice by denying and repressing it to trusting and honoring that voice within, and I became clearer, stronger, and more grounded.

When I finally did leave, I thought I was healed. I ended up attracting another verbal and emotionally abusive relationship with more intensity, which gave me another opportunity to hear an inner dialogue and learn to trust it. This experience showed me that you can leave a situation, but if you haven't fully addressed what is going on inside, the same situation will reoccur, just with a different face. This was an opportunity to dig deep into another layer of healing.

In this particular scenario, I was fortunate that this partner chose to participate in the healing, for which we went to therapy and learned new communication dialogues. I found additional resources including *Heart Centered Therapy* by Alaya Chikly which uses a spiritual dialogue to address physical symptoms, uncover underlying emotions, and integrate wholeness of the inner child within the family lineage and then became a facilitator of the work. I attended a Domestic Violence support group to understand the dynamics and received training as an advocate.

Chapter 7

Although this relationship didn't progress, I had more awareness through these resources than I'd had during the first experience, and knew my breast imbalance had been a gift to guide me toward healing this unhealthy relational pattern and opened a path to what I would do with the first half of my life.

I started educating laypersons and health professionals about the benefits of self-breast massage and herbal oils for better breast health and collaborating with organizations like the American Cancer Society and HerStory. My journey led me to Dr. Laurie Steelsmith, a Hawaii Naturopath who became a mentor along my path.

I received lifestyle wellness support for my breast healing using naturopathic care, supplements, changes in my food choices, and continued to remain mindful of emotional stress. I discovered that the pain was a benign breast imbalance and did diagnostic tests to confirm. My personal healing story and breast oil were featured in Dr. Laurie Steelsmith's book, *Natural Choices for Women's Health* and I was invited to speak about natural ways to optimize breast health at her women's events.

With her recommendation, I then studied and received credentials as a massage therapist, continuing my education in manual lymphatic drainage so I could further my knowledge in how to support women in their health. During this time, I reversed the breast imbalance and felt no more pain.

For the years that followed, I worked with women with benign breast concerns, post-operative healing after breast surgeries, and breast cancer recovery. Holding space for women in their journeys and teaching them how their health challenges became opportunities for them to restore their bodies and rediscover how to love themselves. Women were redefining themselves and their lives. The lifestyle stressors that may have been present at their time of illness, such as divorce, grief, an abusive relationship, or a change in career gave these women the opportunity to start over after their recovery.

Thinking that I was in a better position to find a healthy relationship now, what evolved next became another layer of healing by attracting partners with narcissistic traits. I realized I was attracting these toxic relationships and those from the past because I was seeking love, approval, and validation from outside of myself, which is called Love Addiction. I saw the red flags in these men early but didn't leave, as I thought they would change or I could change them. I built a fantasy in my head based on their potential as they were nice at times. They often told me that what I was asking for in a relationship was too much. I was constantly proving my worth.

Being a highly sensitive and empathetic woman presented more challenges, as I always thought I could fix things, so I was more willing to tune into their needs and pains and than to prioritize my own. I was abandoning myself. Experiencing more feelings of rejection and criticism further impacted my mental health and triggered anxiety in my nervous system like a post traumatic stress experience of my past breast pain. This may have also been the precursor to a later health issue that appeared in 2020 that I was also able to reverse, showing again how much our health can be affected by these relationship dynamics.

In 2015, during my early 40s, the TRUE shift happened. Words said to me by two particular people caused me to take a deep look at myself and question why I was still tolerating and accepting crumbs and not yet in a healthy relationship. Instead of putting blame or focus on what they did or didn't do, I slowly began to release attraction to anyone that was emotionally unavailable and redirect the inquiry on to myself, as I needed to heal my fears of intimacy and abandonment and strengthen my self-esteem. It was time to forgive and give myself the full self-respect I deserved and my loved ones would want for me.

In choosing me, I implemented the NO CONTACT rule with these toxic relationships by creating firm boundaries for myself to avoid further suffering. SELF LOVE AROSE in its truest form and shifted my Energetic Vibration.

Chapter 7

I took that step back to be alone. Then I did the work. I practiced sitting with what I was feeling in my body and emotions; identifying my values, needs and desires; not running to food to alleviate anxiety, and not running towards the toxic relationship, as their attention only provided a temporary relief and lacked true love. I learned to self soothe and be ok with my own company, and not abandon myself anymore. I read books on Codependency, Love Addiction, and Narcissistic Abuse Recovery, and embodied a feeling of greater Self Love through an Equine Coaching experience.

I thought about my greater vision of what I wanted, which was a healthy relationship. I began checking in with myself, and if any person was not in alignment, I said NO Thank You. I also visualized what I wanted to be experiencing in a healthy relationship, to not focus on superficial things, but instead on what I emotionally needed and how I wanted to feel. I continued building my self-nurturing toolkit to make myself a better version of me.

When I wasn't even looking for it, I found a healthy relationship. He is loving, makes me feel safe and heard, and is emotionally available, stable, and a constant in my life.

My mother also loves him (and that is a Big Deal.) I am thankful my soul spoke to me through my breast pain, as it led me down a long path of personal growth and self-discovery of not only healing my health, but owning my power, trusting myself, speaking my voice, and being able to remove myself from relationships that do not support my emotional needs and give me peace. As my great uncle Willie, a Benedictine Monk would say, "Thank those past people, as they were giving you a mirror of what you needed to heal within."

In hindsight, I questioned why I had to go through so many layers of healing. I am reminded of this quote by Barry H. Gillespie: "The path isn't a straight line; it's a spiral. You continually come back to things you thought you understood and see deeper truths."

It has also taken me a long time to feel ok with sharing this, as I was frozen by other people's judgments from the past, which was a reflection of my unconscious wounded healing. Today, I have let that go and learned to love and accept all parts of myself. Doing so has given me a new lens and I know that God's desire is for us to heal, which my soul spoke to me through my body. It would be a disservice for me to not share this, and I hope it inspires women to learn to love and trust themselves.

If you are navigating change and transition, remember that your body can be a powerful guide in expanding the love and care you give to yourself, and through doing this, you can better nurture your emotional well-being by trusting the messages from your body.

Tuning into my body's sensations guided me to my emotions, which led to my creating new lifestyle changes. I took my power back and embraced my worth, then made better choices for myself.

I invite you to explore the three-step self-nurturing process I was guided down. I have found it to be most beneficial when nurturing a health issue, building self-trust in your voice, seeking understanding and alignment in your external and internal environments, and learning to heal stuck emotions.

To the multitude of women who have experienced verbally abusive relationships, other forms of domestic violence, emotionally unavailable partners, unrequited love, or health challenges and recovery, or are navigating other life transitions and are on the path to loving and finding themselves. I see you, support you and invite you to step into your personal power and embrace your worth through the ART of Self-Nurturing- the belief that you are worthy of your own love, care and respect as you rediscover yourself along your journey of Self-Love.

In summary, my personal motto is, "The more you love and care for yourself, the greater the correlation to your optimal health, healthy relationships, and the manifestation of your dreams."

About the Author
Jennifer A. Telford

A Healer, Coach and Teacher, Jennifer A. Telford's dedicated career focuses on guiding women to reclaim their power and embrace their worth by prioritizing self-nurturing.

Her own healing of a breast health imbalance in her 20s inspired her to craft a therapeutic breast massage oil, which was featured in the book, *Natural Choices for Women's Health,* by Dr. Laurie Steelsmith, a Hawaii Naturopath. Her healing also served as a portal through which she embarked on a profound self-love journey, eventually breaking an unhealthy relationship pattern.

For two decades, Jennifer has served as a Massage Therapist specializing in Lymphatic Drainage to support women with Breast Concerns and Breast Cancer Recovery. She holds a Bachelor of Arts in Psychology from Antioch University Los Angeles and a Health Coach Certification and Mastery Level Life Coach Certification from The Health Coach Institute.

Raised on the island of Oahu, Jennifer brings the restorative energy of the Hawaiian islands into her current work as an Integrative Life Coach.

To learn more about Jennifer A. Telford and her embodied healing and empowerment offerings for women, visit **Her Path Her Vision—Transformations for Women by Jennifer Andrea Coaching, a Ho'ano** (*to manifest your vision*) **Wellness subsidiary.**

www.jenniferandreacoaching.com
linktr.ee/jenniferandreacoaching
www.hoano.com

Chapter 8

Life Beyond Hurt

Brandice Scraba

When you come to terms with your own truth, you come to terms with another's truth and the whole world looks completely different. There is no easier way to authentically live than to own your truth and accept it.

I think there are so many different themes to my story. Infidelity. Heartache. Narcissistic abuse. Depression. PTSD. Divorce. But the reality is that the majority of them are not my story to tell. My story is about a woman who lived her life on auto-pilot. Every morning. Every night. Get up. Workout. Get kids to school. Go to work. Run kids to activities. Make supper. Ged kids to bed. Evening time with husband if I was able to stay awake.

This isn't a bad life. Or a boring one at that. But it was not a life. It was a series of events. A series of times and places that made up life. But it was not living. There may have been those moments – intense and powerful moments in life that were more authentic than others. Absolutely. Holding each of my children in my arms for the first time was a moment I'll never forget until the day I die. Or the day I thought I had married my soulmate. Those are days I won't forget. Those are days that have imprinted on me forever and tug at my heart strings and make me feel that life is worth living. But those days were not what the majority of them were like.

The majority of my days were spent justifying my husband's actions. Coming up with excuses and convincing myself that the happily married life was my life – that it defined me and my husband. Maybe I wanted it to. No, I know I wanted it to. I know that's what I believe I had signed up for – the happily ever after. While most of us don't ever sign up thinking that it was not forever, there are those with doubts, but I was not one. I never doubted my heart for a second. I think the most difficult part was someone telling me that I don't know what I want when I knew in my heart that I had made those choices based on love. And to add to that difficulty, someone telling me after years of marriage, three moves, and two children that I don't know what I want. I guess that should have been my very first clue that it was not me who was living the lie.

At 39 years old, I found myself alone with a 12 year old and a 13 year old. After 22 years - more than half my adult life at that time - I found myself without my partner. I was scared. I was vulnerable. I was grieving. I grieved the loss of the family that I thought defined family - a husband, wife, and children. And I grieved the loss of a love that I was under the impression was the greatest of all time. And suddenly everything that I thought was not possible was at my fingertips.

Financial freedom? Definitely not, and this would be the wrong book for that. Financial freedom is a beautiful thing but by no means will it lead you to spiritual realization. An opportunity for an identity shift? 100 percent. An opportunity to be authentically me and love it? 100 percent. An opportunity to make my path my own and enjoy it? 100 percent. An opportunity to live and breathe my own truth? Absolutely.

Suddenly I was no longer validating a man that requires constant validation, and I get to turn the tables and validate myself. What am I good for? What purpose do I have on this earth? Suddenly all of my energy is turned inward and I do more introspection than I

Chapter 8

have done in years, if not decades. Suddenly I am feeling a sense of urgency, a strong and demanding one. What does this mean? What does this look like? This looks like me spending more time with family. This looks like me connecting with old friends that I have not seen in years. This looks like branching out my interests and acquiring new hobbies. This means smiling brighter and laughing deeper. Laughing until my lungs hurt. This means I am no longer on autopilot.

This did not happen immediately. It was not like he moved out and the lightbulb went on. There is a reason why people should not be getting into another relationship right away after a long-term relationship ends. The process of grieving and healing is much more than the healing you would do for a cut or a bruise. The process is longer and even more difficult to navigate, as the process of grief isn't linear, it's dynamic. There are ebbs and flows. There are highs and lows. It's only once the process of grieving really reaches its final stages where you can look at your identity and begin making changes simply for your benefit alone.

I waited nine months before getting into another relationship. It takes nine months to make a human, so that must be enough time to get over a relationship, right? Not exactly. Not at all, actually. Nine months later, I may have understood in my head that I was going through a divorce, but my heart and spirit were still on autopilot. Man. Woman. Children. That is how I grew up and that is exactly what I envisioned my future looking like. So instead of playing the field, dating, having casual sex with strangers, and maybe simply taking the opportunity to focus on anything other than relationships, I found myself right back where I was before: in a committed, long-term relationship.

I swipe right and suddenly I'm back to checking boxes. Financially stable – check. Nice – check. Kids like him – check. Family likes him – check. Suddenly, I found myself dating someone who checked all the boxes. I found myself with someone who was not a narcissist and had the capacity for love and meaning. And I also found myself again . . . checking boxes.

It was not until one night at the curling rink with my new team that it dawned on me that I was maybe not in the right place with this new relationship. The new curling team also has significance. The new curling team was another instrumental step in breaking out of old habits and coming up with something fresh and creative that I have been wanting for awhile but did not say anything out of sheer politeness. I remember telling my team that I just didn't know if I really wanted a relationship. And my teammate looked at me and told me, of course you don't. "You're in your forties. You know who you are. You're an independent woman who wants to exercise her power."

Me? Independent? Powerful? The woman who came out of a 22 year relationship with a controlling narcissist where she felt it was necessary to ask him every time he had a day off of work whether he had any plans to make sure that they would not conflict with plans of her own? That does not sound like an independent and powerful woman. But that was it. I was not that woman anymore. I was not the woman who was constantly asking. I was not the woman walking on eggshells in order to prevent a war. I was not the woman who had to dim her own light just to ensure there was no attention on her. I was suddenly a woman who got to make choices. I was suddenly a woman who felt free to be kind, to be overwhelmingly generous and not worry about the "consequences." I suddenly had the choice to be whoever I wanted to be.

This sounds like the easiest thing in the entire universe when in reality, one of the hardest things to do in life is to turn off your autopilot. I don't mean cruise control; that's easy - you put your foot on the brake and suddenly you are no longer on cruise control. However, in real life that is not so easy. It is not easy to tell your boyfriend that literally checks all the boxes that you're not deeply in love and ready to commit. It is not easy to tell your ex-husband that he is a narcissistic idiot that keeps hurting his children. It is not easy to tell your family that you will not be available that weekend because you need the weekend to yourself. It is easy to nod your head and smile. It is easy to go with the flow. It is easy to make the choices that make

Chapter 8

other people happy. It is easy to put a smile on your face and play pretend.

Living your life authentically is not playing pretend. Living your life authentically is eating, sleeping, breathing your life to the fullest. Living your life authentically is thinking, damn, that sunset tonight was gorgeous. Living your life means feeling completely exhausted after those 19km of walking. Living your life authentically means that you will not look back and think, why did I waste all those years. 39 years were enough to waste. I was not wasting a day more.

Did my life change drastically? Probably not to anyone who saw me in the grocery store. Probably not to the neighbor who came over to push my snow. Probably not to the coach who coached my son in soccer. To my family? To my friends? To my children? Definitely. Suddenly those hugs with my nieces last a bit longer. Suddenly when my mom asks what I am doing for the weekend, I can give her a concrete answer rather than waiting to see what she says first. Suddenly laughter during Girls' Night lasts the whole night. Suddenly hugs and deep, profound conversations are ever present. Suddenly I am refinishing a piece of furniture, working with my hands, something that has never appealed to me before, and something I would have never believed that I would be able to do.

One of the most surprising things in this journey of healing and growing was becoming able to be there for other people suffering similar trauma. One day I was in the Dollar Store shopping for the kids when I answered my phone to hear a small voice, holding back tears, say, "It's me." I could have come up with an excuse – *I'm in the middle of shopping. I can't talk right now.* Instead I left the store and sat in my car and told her, "It's going to be ok." I then went into the disclaimer. You may not sleep properly for eight months. You may cry in the middle of your shift. You may question your every waking moment. But you got this and you're going to be ok. Never in a million years did I think the disaster I was would become the person that others respected enough to come to when their house of cards came tumbling down. I also never thought I would hear, "I can't believe you are ok." or "I cannot believe how well you are doing." I tell every one of my clients when they are faced with a very very difficult situation, "Rome was not built in a day." And it wasn't. Self healing and self worth are no different.

Was it one thing in particular? One thought? One action? Ironically, like autopilot, it was a series of events. A series of changes. A meeting with a spiritual guide. A book called Letting That Shit Go. A couple trips to the lake with the paddleboard and good friends. Living authentically can look a lot like autopilot, after all; it is a series of events that don't look any different. The difference is the intention. The difference is in the conscious effort. The difference is that your life now has meaning and you want your activities to be meaningful. The difference is that you are making choices based on what you want and what makes your heart soar. It does not mean that you won't be stuck doing things you don't want to, like paying taxes and working. It does mean that you are living a life of intention, a life of meaning.

I was never the one in my relationships to fix or build anything. That was always the husband's/boyfriend's role. I never felt that I was even capable of such things, even though I grew up on a farm where I had spent countless hours helping my dad and when at one point in my life, I could pick up a 9/16 wrench out of the bunch by memory. I became so distant from myself and my abilities that I literally felt compelled to stick to the things I could handle without a second thought, like making a meal, looking after the children, or cleaning. Seven months after my husband moved out, I successfully completed a firearms course. I knew that being legal meant my daughter could keep her guns in our home. Ten months later, I refinished a vanity that had been passed down to me from my Baba. I spent hours and hours of meticulous work on it. And loved every second. Nearly two years later, I mudded, sanded, and painted the walls of my basement living room to fill the gaping holes left after my ex-husband removed all his dead animal heads. Filling those holes, working with my hands, and watching the progress was no Ghost moment, I assure you, but it was pretty damn close. Seeing the end result and knowing that it was my hands that had crafted it

Chapter 8

was an incredible feeling. Two and a half years later, I ordered a giant tarp for an enormous tarp shed to ensure a second vehicle for my daughter, who will be driving in less than a year, would be protected. I called the company and allowed the salesperson to go through each option as I weighed the pros and cons of each to understand what I needed and what best suited us. Then I hauled the 115-pound box to my vehicle because I didn't want the Loomis guy doing it. And then with the assistance of the kids and minimal directions, and nearly six hours, the finished product was there, a new, fresh-looking tarp shed next to my home, perfectly matching the siding. These seem like little things - and in reality they are - but these are the things that before connecting with myself, believing in myself, and number one, trusting myself - would never have happened. I'm not saying that after you divorce, you'll suddenly gain the handyman skills you'd never had before. What I am saying is that coming to believe in and trust yourself is the most self-satisfying process you will ever experience, even if you make a wrong decision, even if it does not turn out right. Knowing you trusted yourself and your instincts is far more valuable than any trade or education.

It was not until I started living authentically that I could truly reflect on what my life had looked like before. In the moments of my past, I had been happy. Looking back now, I can see how much of my life had been what I'd thought it should look like - what I'd wanted it to look like. By living authentically, I regained friends. By living authentically, I drew people in that I might not have even talked to before. By living authentically, I connected with my children on a deeper and more emotional level. By living authentically, I was approached by family and people who have been through similar experiences, by people who are challenged by what to do next and by the staggering waves of grief that hit when a relationship ends. By living authentically and sharing my truth, people were able to see that there is life beyond hurt, confusion, and grief.

I had a good friend. A good dear friend that I loved and respected. A friend so connected that we were often able to finish each other's sentences. A friend that one day no longer seemed to be part of my life anymore and I did not understand why, so when that friend later tried to reconnect, I offered her what I thought she had offered me years earlier: a cold shoulder. A year after my ex-husband moved out, the fog started lifting from my brain and I realized that my friend hadn't abandoned me. My friend needed to walk away because she could not watch as I announced my pregnancy to the world just days after I found out that my husband had been cheating on me not even nine months into our marriage. My friend had to walk away. My friend couldn't watch things unfold as they did. I will never say that I regret not walking away from my marriage right then. Walking away at that time would have meant that today, I would not have my son. My son and daughter are the light of my life, and they are my reason for trying, for breathing, and for simply trying to be the best human possible. I let my friend know that I understood why she had done what she did, and that it was ok. And I received the most beautiful response I could have ever anticipated, but that is another story.

There is life beyond your darkest days. There is life beyond the hurt, the pain, and the confusion. I heard a saying recently that struck me: "As long as there is breath, there is hope." And as long as I am on this earth, I will continue to have hope. Hope that one day, my children will understand that they do not ever have to stand in the shadow of another human being. Hope that they will love themselves freely and unconditionally. Hope that they will make choices based on love and authenticity, not on norms and regulations. Hope that one day they will see that no matter what life throws at them, no matter the hurt, no matter how hard it gets, that they will always have a choice.

About the Author
Brandice Scraba

Brandice Scraba is a firm believer in resilience and embraces an "I can and I will" mindset. She aspires to instill the importance of self-love in her two children. By overcoming challenges and fears of inadequacy, Brandice broke free from autopilot living.

Throughout her career, she has dedicated herself to helping children and families, a passion she continues to fulfill in her current government role. Brandice's roots are deeply embedded in the importance of family and she has become open to the reality that "family" comes in many forms.

Brandice is fulfilling her lifelong dream of becoming an author, sharing her inspiring journey to support those in difficult situations where they do not feel they have a choice . Her story exemplifies the power of self-love and resilience, a guiding light for others seeking a fulfilling life.

Chapter 9

Coming Into My Power and Finding My Voice: It's Not About Finding the Right Path, It's About Finding the Path That's Right for You

Belinda Djurasovic

I believe that a lot of people seek the same purpose in life, happiness, which if they seek more, will lead to fulfilment. Along my journey I have learnt that happiness can look very different from person to person, but ultimately once you truly connect with yourself, it looks nothing like what you first thought it was. Along the journey we can sometimes avoid facing emotions or situations that we fear, which in the short term protects us, but long term can have the opposite effect by preventing us from reaching the dream destination of happiness. The mind will always lean towards seeking pleasure and avoiding pain. I have learnt to lean into instead of leaning out of my emotions, wants, and most importantly, needs.

Reflecting back over my life, if someone had asked me what lessons do I wish I could have skipped over along my journey, I would say, none. The highs and lows in life all play a vital role in shaping who we are as people, but also give us that fire in the belly to fight for the life we want for ourselves, our children, and future generations. By pulling wisdom out of my experiences, I have come to stand in my power and have a voice. This is one of my proudest transformations.

Through my own transformational journey, I developed tools to become a better parent, friend, and friend to myself, with more patience and tolerance, and by approaching life from a place of understanding and curiosity instead of judgement.

From a young age I felt like I had no voice. I didn't even have the confidence to speak up even if I wanted to, at home, in school, around friends, and later in life at work. I don't ever remember not feeling anxiety, also known as fearing the future. Most children of my generation had the type of parents who would do anything for us and they dedicated themselves to being providers, but we didn't have the space to express or process our emotions, which for me is probably what I really needed. As an anxious child, I always feared getting punished by our strict parents, the things that could happen, and things that hadn't even happened, like how I would pay bills when I grew up, how would I know how to be an adult, and other things a young child shouldn't even be worrying about. I felt like I was always in a hypervigilant state, not knowing what was coming next, and I perceived everything as a threat. I know now I was also carrying some ancestral trauma from many generations before me. It's likely that even my genes were carrying some of those experiences and anxieties, affecting how I felt, how I saw the world, and how I thought about myself. The worries I carried were not always my own. To release what didn't belong to me, from a long line of people who came before me, I accepted the past and did meditative and somatic practices both on my own and with a trained trauma facilitator to identify fears, shame, anxieties, and limitations, then handing them back to my ancestors by connecting with them, envisioning releasing these things, and creating an energy release. Doing this also ensured that the trauma will end with my generation.

Although there have been a number of difficult times in my life, the not-so-great patterns I developed during my childhood, and especially during my teenage years, shaped me and all my experiences

Chapter 9

until I came to stand in my power as an evolved version of my true self. It's almost like I have been reprogrammed to seek support rather than remain silent, and further feed my drive to find what fulfills me, which is helping others step towards their own happiness and the desires coming from their souls.

Over three decades ago, at the start of my teenage years, any feeling of safety I'd had was completely taken away and my voice was repeatedly diminished when a male neighbour a few years older than me started molesting me. At first it was infrequent, but over time it became a regular occurrence. He would watch for when nobody was home and despite my best attempts to secure the house and hide, he would find a way into our home. He would follow me from shopping centres, from the bus stop, or on my way to school and attack me. I had nowhere to hide, nowhere to escape to, so I never felt safe. My body would go into a complete freeze state when he was attacking me. I now know this was my body shutting down in response to sensing danger and my nervous system trying to appease and keep me safe. I blamed myself for the abuse by telling myself that if I'd had the courage to un-freeze, yell, and fight back, it would have stopped. I felt terrified and every day I became even more hypervigilant, always scanning my environment, always expecting something bad to happen. I had no voice to speak up and tell anybody, as I'd feared there would be repercussions from my abuser. The anxiety took over as a perceived danger about speaking out.

After two and a half years, I reached breaking point. I felt like everything around me was crumbling. I was fighting with my parents and feared my future even more. I needed it to stop, so I gathered every bit of courage I had and ran away. For a young girl who already felt no safety within her world, this was terrifying, but it was better than being in my current life. I am proud of myself for having that courage. I felt so much guilt, as I knew my family would be worried, but I didn't see any alternative. As a conditioned people pleaser and someone who feared that others would feel awkward hearing about what was happening, I didn't feel I could speak up about what was truly going on. Instead, I left and took on the burden myself. As a mother, even with how much healing I have done, I still struggle to think about any child carrying such a burden and not feeling safe in the world.

A few weeks after running away from home, I was found by the police. They took me to the police station and an officer took me into a room for an interview. Even at the time I realised this was a "chat" that runaway teens received to scare them off from running away again. I opened up to the officer about being molested and that this is why I ran away. I thought I would finally receive the support I needed. Unfortunately it went the other way. He asked me if I would like to press charges and take the matter to court. For a moment I felt so empowered. But when I responded with yes, he proceeded to tell me there was no point because there is no evidence, and it would be my word against his and hard to prove in court. He essentially said whatever he could to talk me out of progressing further.

This is where I stopped feeling supported to speak up. That officer just swept the last two and a half years under the carpet. My family supported me by selling our family home and moving away, but they never spoke with me about anything. I never mentioned it again because I felt uncomfortable within myself. The police officer wouldn't even support me, and telling him had taken every bit of courage I'd had left to speak up. I had no words left in me.

Over the decades that followed, I felt brief moments of motivation to open up to people about what I'd gone through in my teenage years, but my doing so was often met with silence because people didn't know what to say, and then I felt uncomfortable thinking that I'd made them feel uncomfortable. Or at least, that was my perception. I'm not even sure what response I needed, maybe just a firm hug to bring my body back into a feeling of safety, or maybe to be asked questions, rather than having my fears of speaking about it validated.

It is not ok to abuse women, it is not ok for women to not feel supported, and it is not ok for authorities to not listen. In 2023 I contacted the police station that interviewed me all those years ago and requested a record of my interview. I was told that they were unable to locate a file on me. I wasn't sure I trusted them and felt a little invisible when I received this response. I'm not sure I need to see the police report, but I did need to speak up and say that the way they as authorities had undermined a teenage girl was not ok.

Throughout my life, I developed a pattern of denying my worth, pleasing people to make sure they wouldn't reject me, having no voice in my relationships, and seeking validation from the wrong kind of people. I didn't even have the courage to speak up in a restaurant if I was given the wrong meal. My anxiety just kept growing and so did additional significant and challenging life events with friends and family. I didn't have the tools or strength to process them as they happened. I had my first breakdown in my early 20s which shook me to my core. I could barely function from anxiety and started experiencing panic attacks. I also developed digestive issues and depression, couldn't eat or sleep properly, and disconnected from myself and the world. I covered up missing so much work with excuses and a fake smile to the world. The effects stayed for many more years to come and led to a roller coaster of good times and a string of burnouts and breakdowns.

Although I had seen counsellors and psychologists and had tried medication, chronic anxiety always lurked in the background, and nothing seemed to help. The real start of my turning point in my journey to finding relief began when I read the book *The Monk Who Sold His Ferrari* by Robin Sharma. I read a passage about rather than looking at a brick wall and seeing the imperfections of one brick that's not aligned, instead looking at and appreciating the whole wall . Something about this spoke to me. Maybe I wasn't broken - I didn't *need* to be a perfectly aligned brick wall. I felt hopeful for the first time. I didn't know it until many years later, but this likely started my spiritual journey of feeling deeper within myself and realising I wasn't broken. I found myself seeking out small glimmers every day and letting go of never feeling good enough or trying to make everything perfect. Seeking out glimmers means scanning your world for things that bring you joy instead of being triggered or looking for things that could be wrong, like noticing how beautiful the autumn leaves are when the afternoon sun hits them. My mind opened to a whole new world that I had never even noticed before.

That one passage from a book started rewiring my brain and soul from seeing everything as a threat to instead seeking positivity and gratitude for everything life had given me. I read my first book about neuroplasticity and found comfort in learning that the brain can in fact rewire itself, so I wasn't designed to feel and think negatively forever. I started to learn how to connect with myself, look within, and ultimately create a whole new energy field around me. Instead of attracting negative experiences, I shifted my mindset and started to manifest what I wanted by realising that life is a mirror of our thoughts and I am where my attention is. None of this happened overnight and my path was a long one. It fast tracked when a spiritual healer opened my eyes to listening to the messages I was receiving and acting on them, which shifted my frequency and built the energy that I live in everyday. Thoughts and behaviours affect the rhythms in our bodies, which makes complete sense since every cell in our bodies is made up of energy and we are each a living energy field; even science tells us that! Where energy flows, life follows. But I was still being triggered, and lifelong stress and anxiety were starting to manifest as chronic pain, adrenal fatigue, and chronic fatigue. Whilst I know now about mind-body illness and prioritise my wellness daily, that was another lesson I had to learn on my own.

Leaving my corporate job was a pivotal event in my transformational journey. The more I learned to connect with my colourful true self, the more disconnected I felt to my beige office cubicle. I felt like a square peg in a round hole as I felt triggered by the environment, toxic egos, and constant pressure to perform. After one of my bosses bullied me, I completely lost my mojo for the corporate environment. At the time I was not yet strong enough within my own healing journey to shield myself from her belittling behaviour toward me, which led to my having another breakdown. I am still

Chapter 9

reminded of this every day, as it gave me tinnitus, a permanent ringing in the ears caused by chronic stress. Would I have been able to prevent getting this condition had I found my voice earlier in life and been able to advocate for myself throughout my life and career? More than likely. But I feel like that was the final part of my awakening, the learning that I needed to chase something greater. I made up any excuse I could to avoid promotions and more than ever felt like I didn't belong. Even though I was a high achiever at work, which I now recognise was just people pleasing behaviour, my soul wanted to be free from that. I tried very hard to fly under the radar until I became pregnant and left my corporate job. Walking out of my beige cubicle for the very last time and knowing I would never be back felt so liberating.

Nothing could have prepared me for the path motherhood then took me on. Whilst my anxiety motor was already humming in the background, after my daughter was born, it escalated to severe post-natal anxiety by my baby daughter's colic. I could not put her down at all and she screamed in pain all day. My concerns for her health were dismissed by various doctors. Once again I was not being heard or listened to. Still I persisted and found a specialist who listened, and very soon afterward, I had a happy and settled baby. I couldn't say the same about myself.

However, my daughter again became constantly unsettled. I had not healed from the post-natal anxiety yet and felt so much guilt when she saw me dysregulated and being triggered by her inability to control her behaviour. No young child should control their behaviour, it is their communications that should be met with curiosity and empathy for how they are experiencing the world around them. My daughter was like a mirror showing me what I had not yet healed and still needed to work on, or re-parent within myself. Had I not had a child, I would likely have been able to keep it together and carry on, missing the final pieces of my healing journey. Even I could see that my dark and heavy energy was impacting my little family.

As a parent of a child who sometimes has complex emotional and sensory needs I need to dig deep each day. It can be exhausting and feel like a never-ending learning curve, but it's also a wonderfully fulfilling experience to guide these brilliant children who are sensitive to a world that is not set up for them. What I have learnt is that through all the tools, therapies, and strategies, the most beneficial thing for helping my daughter get better is me being better. She deeply feels the energy I create within myself and in our home, which drives me onto a never ending quest to seek an embodied process to fulfill my desires and happiness.

Before I'd even known that my child had additional needs, I was ignoring the advice of others that she was just in a phase that would pass. The pattern of not having a voice was being broken. Tuning in to my intuition about what my daughter needed, I dove deep into learning about the nervous system, being with emotions instead of shutting them down, regulating myself when I felt triggered, and incorporating wellness practices throughout my day. What I didn't realise at the time was that I was actually educating myself about what I needed: true embodiment. Each time I was triggered as a parent and became reactive was actually my own unmet needs triggering me, like what I'd needed myself as a child, but had never opened up and expressed.

Once I heard the phrase "breaking the cycle," I couldn't un-hear it. Knowing that some of my patterns and fears I was carrying were not my own, I used this phrase as motivation to heal myself. By changing my energy, I am not only being a good example for my daughter, I'm also healing the generations before me. By breaking the patterns of not speaking up, by feeling emotions and processing them instead of stuffing them away and being brave enough to be a female leader, my patterns and the patterns of the past would not be passed on through me to future generations.

I became an advocate for reframing thoughts and emotions by truly embodying them, as this creates the necessary clarity and change to create whatever our hearts desire. Through my journey I had been fortunate to experience somatic therapy to guide me through the last

Chapter 9

of my deep, unprocessed emotions from traumatic events. I have learned how to connect and listen to myself to create the life I want, but most importantly, I have gained the confidence to know that I can quickly bring myself back from a dysregulated state and process any limiting beliefs that arise so they won't hold me back.

If I knew these answers years earlier, my own journey to healing may have been much quicker, but I choose to not focus on that, as my journey led to so many lessons and to discovering my purpose to help others. I couldn't have done this until I first walked the path myself. Today I have the tools, mindset, and simple daily practices to help myself feel like there is a village behind me every day, freeing me from chronic anxiety and giving me a new sense of confidence and true self-worth. I have learnt that you can't talk your way into believing something, you need to embody it, because your body needs to feel it.

My physical body is still catching up to my healing journey, but I am confident that the last of the chronic pains and fatigue will subside. The body really does remember; memories and stored emotions impact our whole being, so looking after my soul and nervous system has become my priority. I have replaced stressful situations and thoughts with positive experiences for my heart and body, teaching my body to become addicted to calm and coherence.

From understanding comes acceptance. When I understood why I felt the way I did and why my body and mind reacted the way they did, real healing began. I worked with it, not against it, and didn't just accept that this was "just the way I am." I removed those words from my vocabulary and no longer identify with them.

The journey of transformation or healing is not linear. Sometimes it feels like progress and sometimes it feels like swimming against a current. I've learnt that there is no final destination, as self-discovery is a never ending path. The deeper you dive in, the more you discover, and the more people come into your life to introduce you to new ways of thinking, the more you are given new opportunities to be led in many different ways. It's not about finding the right path, it's about finding the path that's right for you. Nobody has had the exact same healing experience as I have, and yet, over time I have built my tribe of people who understand me, look after me, and show me how to be a better person, and who long to help each other navigate their way. Nobody needs to walk their path alone, especially on their own unique path to happiness.

I have learned to be a disruptor, determined to make sure no one shapes my journey again. Only I can tell the world what my destination will be.

About the Author
Belinda Djurasovic

Belinda Djurasovic's journey of transformation led her to discovering her true voice and healing both her own pain and the pain passed down through generations. Through this powerful process, she became attuned to the internal "voices" that guided her, unlocking a world of self-connection and boundless possibilities. Her profound experience fueled a desire to assist other women and become a role model for her young daughter, igniting a passion for nourishing her nervous system, body, and soul.

After breaking free from the cycle of burnout, breakdowns, and people-pleasing, Belinda dedicated herself to following her purpose of helping others. Her mission is to empower women and mothers by showing them how to unlock their full potential and embrace a life of thriving, rather than merely surviving. In 2023, she founded Brass Village as a platform for coaching and mentoring others on this transformative journey.

If you're interested in connecting with Belinda and learning more about her work, visit https://brassvillage.com.au.
Follow Belinda on Instagram @brass_village: brass_village
Follow Belinda on Facebook: Brass Village

Chapter 10

Patterns and Potential: Unearthing Change at the Birthing Cave

Nicolette Halladay

In the heart of Sedona, Arizona nestled amidst ancient red sandstone formations, lies a sanctuary of transformation - the Birthing Cave. This chapter of my journey was not merely a trek through picturesque landscapes; it was an exploration of life's intricate patterns, a revelation of trust, and an awakening to the power of breaking free from entrenched cycles.

Our odyssey in Sedona brimmed with anticipation and camaraderie. Conversations intertwined dreams of business ventures, podcasts, and a co-facilitated retreat, intermingled with personal tales of navigating divorce and crafting a life guided by adventure, abundance, and grace.

Mary, my dear friend and guide through this expedition, surprised me with an invitation to the Birthing Cave - a rarity for visitors. Her certainty about something special awaiting us ignited curiosity and set the tone for an experience beyond the ordinary.

Dense red sandstone padded the trail. The thought of the giant red boulders breaking down over thousands and even millions of years into the finely textured dust that was now under our feet was awe-inspiring. The views of the vibrant red stone formations in the distance, lush green foliage, and royal blue sky encapsulated the beauty of this sacred land.

We hiked along the trail and into the cave. We only passed a few people along the way. The last people we passed let us know that we would get to enjoy the cave in privacy because there was no one else up there. Later, Mary would tell me how unique that is—that this is a popular Sedona destination usually experienced with strangers who also want to share the potency of the birthing cave. But the birthing cave had something special in store for me—something she wanted me to experience privately with my dear friend Mary guiding me along the way.

We stepped into the hollow rock formation, and without a thought, I quickly jumped out of my shoes, slipping off my socks, my bare feet landing on the slick, glazed rock. My skin connected deeply with the wisdom of this ancient rock. My bare feet allowed me to quickly scurry up the rock formation, like bare feet climbing up a slide, suctioning to the smooth surface beneath them.

Mary pulled out her camera and said, "The first thing I want to do is take pictures of you." I posed with my hand on my hip and then both hands pointing to the sky as I looked up and took in the massiveness of this place and this moment.

Mary pointed to a large notch in the stone above me, a carved-out nook that could fit a person, and said, "When Bridget was here, she went up there." Before a thought could even cross my mind, my feet ran up the slick rock. Mary said, "You have to be bare-footed, which you already are." I did not stop to consult Mary; I didn't stop to think about how I would get down. I zip and zagged along the rock, lifting myself into the hole with my arms as I climbed into the opening.

I sat perched inside the hole in this stone wall, observing the view from this unique perspective. Mary continued to take pictures of me. I stood up to find that my height was the perfect size for the opening. "She doesn't let everyone up there, you know." Mary said, referring to the Birthing Cave. "Few people experience it; I never

Chapter 10

have." she said. I sat back down to take in the moment, absorbing the gravity of what she was saying. "Not everyone gets to come up here," I thought, to the womb of the birthing cave. I sat in her womb, to the place she had beckoned me, placed my hands on my heart, and gave gratitude for this precious gift.

I started to look down and realized that getting down would be tricky. I had lifted myself into the hole, and the idea of turning around and coming down that way felt scary. The distance between me and the ledge, the significant drop below the ridge, and the hard, slick rock below was sinking in. My heart started quickening, beating harder in my chest. I began to lower myself down but didn't like the angle, so I propped myself back up. My heart pounded. The realization that this was my life and that this was a pattern that I had experienced time and time again. A quick and enthusiastic start - anything is possible - propelled my endeavors to an expedited incline only to reach a height and a new perspective and let the thoughts of fear, failure, and doubt seep in and derail me. Slowing down my endeavors and sometimes stopping me in my tracks altogether. I voiced this to Mary. "This is my life, you know" I explained, BIG, beautiful beginnings, only to doubt my ability to maneuver through the ending." She nodded, letting me process what was coming through.

Mary pointed out a few spots where she thought I could move. I lowered myself onto the ledge with her instruction. I sat, my belly pressed against the rock, my bare feet on the narrow ledge, and my back facing the drop between where I was and where I was going. I was on the ridge but couldn't see the path down. I took deep belly breaths into my chest to slow down my breathing. I patted the rock and asked her to show me the next step. The grip for my hand caught my attention, and then the flat spot in the rock for my foot. I had enough space to turn my body around. My heart kept pounding. I patted the smooth stone, thanking her for guiding me. Mary and I talked about different possibilities and ways I could go. I asked the rock again for guidance and found the best next step. My descent was as slow, precise, and meticulous as my intuitively quick and free climb up. Each step was carefully thought through, with support from Mary and the Birthing Cave herself guiding my way. But ultimately, it was me. I chose the next best step: when to stop and when to hurry. I allowed my body to know the way and safely made my way down.

I got to the bottom, and I let out a resounding cry of relief. Moans of emotion left my body. The emotional release was anchored more in the realization that had just played out in this physical reality then in the experience itself. I knew I would make it down that rock. I never doubted my agility, strength, or ability to maneuver down it. The rock challenged me; it asked me to see this pattern that continued to play out in my life and gave me this physical experience to see it through a new lens. And that shook me to my core. I knew it was meaningful, but I couldn't quite put it into words. It felt like there were more revelations to come that I couldn't see yet.

Mary and I lay on the smooth, cool rock, staring up at the opening at the top of the cave. She said, "Do you see what that is?" pointing to what looked like a vagina in the rock—the vaginal opening right above the womb, where I had sat just moments earlier.

We walked back on the soft sand path in solitude and silence. With the light Sedona breeze across our skin, as the sun lowered in the sky, highlighting different hues of oranges, yellows, greens, and browns, we breathed in this shared experience.

On the drive back to camp, Mary got a call. While she was talking on the phone, the second ball dropped for me. Visions of the births of each of my girls play out in my mind's eye. Each of my daughters had gone into fetal distress during their delivery, followed by panic and the need to get them out quickly. With my first daughter, Aleah, my body had dilated enough to allow her to come naturally (enough) through the birth canal, with the doctor's forceps squeezing her head and violently pulling out her limp body. My younger two girls required surgery to be removed quickly enough to be safe. Each delivery started peaceful and smooth, leaving me feeling capable and like anything was possible, but would inevitably escalate into

Chapter 10

panic and uncertainty. My thoughts carried me to a new thread of my birth, where I, too, went into fetal distress. My mother intuitively knew that something wasn't right, insisting the planned cesarean happen immediately - she was right; the umbilical cord was tangled, and I was slowly suffocating. The realization that this was a pattern that I had just played out in the birthing cave. The quick and hopeful beginning, followed by panic and uncertainty, always ended with a happy ending and loads of support from earth and heavenly angels.

When I arrived at my camp, messages from my two younger daughters came through: "Mommy, I miss you" from my youngest and "Hi Mom, how are you?" from my middle daughter. My youngest daughter communicates regularly when not with me, but my older daughter is less likely to. It's as if they felt it, too. The cord I had healed. The pattern interrupted. They don't have to maneuver through such a choppy existence, and they can move smoothly through new projects. They might not have to become paralyzed with fear like I have so many times in my creative and professional pursuits. They might get to feel nurtured as they move through the different stages. Their nervous system can be calm and comforting.

I have carried this birth trauma since my first earthly breath, and it has impacted everything I have brought into existence ever since. Whether that was human life, business expansion, a creative project, or a new chapter in life, the path would follow a similar fate.

As I grapple with the depth of this realization, it intertwines with the concept of embracing momentum through bold movement. It's akin to surrendering to life's currents without hesitation - a daring leap into uncharted territories, unbound by fear or doubt. This courageous forward step is transformative, steering us towards unexplored potentials and new horizons.

Unveiling the power of uninhibited action, this momentum sparks an energy that permeates our pursuits, infusing them with vitality and fervor. It defies stagnation, nurturing growth in personal, professional, and spiritual realms.

Moving decisively, unburdened by hesitation, breaks self-imposed boundaries, affirming our ability to navigate challenges and carve our destinies. This momentum fosters resilience and adaptability, enabling us to thrive amid uncertainty.

It becomes a catalyst for fearless innovation, encouraging us to explore new ideas and challenge norms. Each bold step forward initiates an unstoppable ripple effect, redefining our trajectory and shaping a narrative teeming with limitless possibilities. It fuels personal evolution, societal transformation, and a world where boundless potential thrives.

May your unhesitant movement be the harbinger of a momentum that propels you toward the extraordinary, unraveling a tapestry of innovation, growth, and unbounded success.

Life, in its ever-unfolding narrative, presents us with subtle clues, whispers of wisdom, and opportunities for growth. These clues manifest in myriad forms - encounters, experiences, or the serene whispers of nature. When we attune ourselves to these clues, when we are receptive and open, they become guideposts illuminating our path to evolution.

The ascent into the Birthing Cave mirrored life's spirited beginnings, where enthusiasm and potential surge forth. As I perched within the cave's inner sanctum, life unveiled a metaphor - an invitation to observe, to listen, and to decipher the echoes resonating within.

The descent became an intentional unraveling of repetitive cycles, reminiscent of life's patterns. Each step down was an acknowledgment - a conscious effort to heed life's subtle clues and break free from ingrained cycles. It echoed the transformative power found in the acceptance of these hints, leading to growth and evolution.

Lying within the cool embrace of the cave, the metaphorical womb, life's teachings echoed louder. It reminded me that life constantly presents us with lessons, hidden within its subtle nuances. Yet, it's our willingness, our openness to receive and interpret these messages, that determines our growth and evolution.

Chapter 10

This awakening marks a transformative juncture - an invitation to break free from past constraints and birth new narratives, unshackled by the chains of old patterns.

So, dear reader, as you navigate your path, may you embrace the echoes resonating within you. Recognize the power to break free from repetitive cycles, enabling the birth of fresh narratives painted by liberated spirits.

Come and be part of our retreat in Sedona, where you'll delve into the teachings of the Birthing Cave - a sanctuary for exploration, rejuvenation, and the creation of fresh starts. It's a place to unravel patterns, foster new ideas, and build connections with kindred spirits. May these echoes lead you on a liberating journey, and may the whispers of the Birthing Cave light your way toward unexplored beginnings.

About the Author
Nicolette Halladay

Making waves in the publishing world, bestselling author and publisher Nicolette Halladay is the CEO of Inspired Hearts Publishing. A storyteller, a publisher, a purpose-seeker... She is here to help entrepreneurs, creatives, and change-makers find the courage to be seen and heard.

After spending 5 years behind the scenes supporting other businesses as a virtual assistant, she decided it was time to stop hiding. She felt called to help women, who had stories just like her, take center stage by becoming published authors.

She's on a mission to create a world where aspiring leaders can become published authors without gatekeepers—using the pen to empower and amplify women's voices one book at a time!

Embracing life's adventures with her three wild and wonderful daughters, this Colorado native is a lover of all things outdoors and is passionate about connecting with others.

Follow her journey to inspire, empower, and equip the next generation of thought leaders!

Connect with Nicolette:
Website: www.nicolettehalladay.com
Facebook: www.facebook.com/nikki.richardsonhalladay
Instagram: www.instagram.com/nicolettehalladay111

Chapter 11

Are You There, God? I Sure Freaking Hope So.

Erica Hurtt

H*ow prayer saved my life and led me back to God*

Belief in God can seem like an indulgent and convenient fantasy best suited for children. This was certainly the way I felt years ago when I sat in my car contemplating suicide on a warm spring afternoon outside a Washington, DC-area metro station.

Nothing made sense. I had the ingredients for what's supposed to be a good American life - a college degree or two, a house, a career, nights out on the town with pretty friends, an attractive partner, trips to tropical destinations, and a 401(k) plan. But everything felt empty and pointless. How did I get here? How could I escape these feelings? These were questions that pinged around my brain like a fly trapped in a glass jar, creating fear, insecurity, and a persistent sense of impending doom.

It would take me several years to find the answers to what was spawning these feelings of anxiety, depression, and hopelessness. It turned out escape was not what I needed, but rather connection in order to find peace, serenity, and self love.

The concept of God was introduced to me by my parents at an early age. Some of my earliest memories are of a pink, pocket-sized Bible I received as a gift and a seemingly ubiquitous figurine found in many households in the 1980s of a boy and a girl kneeling together in prayer. I cherished this porcelain depiction of what I imagined to be me and my older brother and kept it atop my bedroom dresser for many years.

As a child, I attended Sunday School and said bedtime prayers. Each night those prayers included a list of people I asked God to bless, from my parents, to my brothers, to neighborhood friends. I always ended by asking God to bless me and closed by stating, "I love Erica." This simple declaration at the end of each day unleashed a feeling of overwhelming self love.

I felt a sense of peace in believing someone was in the sky, or way out in the universe, looking out for me. Someone strong and all powerful. Someone who loved me just as I was and made me for a specific purpose. This was especially helpful when things didn't make sense. When adults who were supposed to love and protect me instead hurt me. When classmates teased me for my freckles or made fun of my last name or a clothing choice.

As I sat in my car decades later outside that metro station contemplating death, I wondered, what happened to that self love? What happened to that peace? Where was that faithful little girl?

By the end of my elementary school days, church was no longer a feature of my life. Soccer games and other social activities took priority on the weekends. I stopped saying prayers. I started on a path of not believing, a path that later led to many dark and empty places, winding and turning for years.

As an adolescent, I was easily influenced and eager to please and gain acceptance. I grew up with a lot of fear. Fear of disappointing my parents, teachers, coaches, and really anyone I encountered. Fear of being left out. Fear of being disliked. Fear of financial insecurity. I was like a seashell tossing in the waves and going wherever I was pushed.

Chapter 11

Before iPods, Spotify, and even 5-disc CD changers, I loved cruising in my 1990 red Toyota Celica, rocking along as one of my favorite tunes pulsated from the crappy stereo system. With the wind in my hair and lyrics on my lips, driving always gave me a sense of freedom and control, but even that was short lived.

On countless occasions, midway through one of my favorite jams, I would find myself wondering if there was a better song, one that I liked even more, playing on another radio station. I typically drove with my left hand on the steering wheel, the right gingerly poised on the gear shift, hovering over the station preset buttons. It was challenging to be content with that moment and that song. I always felt the need to change the channel to see what else was out there. It was the same way with jobs, hobbies, boyfriends, and other situations: any sense of contentment was usually crowded out by the never-ending question, *But what if there is something better?*

This sense of unease was always lurking. Even as a child, a voice nagged in the back of mind, pulling me out of the present. I wasn't necessarily an unhappy child, but I was preoccupied with and consumed by how others might be viewing the circumstances I was dealing with or decisions I had made, or frankly with how they were feeling versus my own sense of contentment. My focus on what *could be* or *should be* left no chance for me to appreciate the here and now and what life had already given me. It left me feeling untethered, floating in the ether, waiting for the next set of "something better" to give me the sense of worth and contentment I desperately craved.

By focusing on the past, future, what I was missing in that moment, or what others thought of me, I struggled to stay in the moment. I never felt ok or content. I had a serious case of FOMO before FOMO was a thing.

From a very early age, I knew something was missing inside me. It wasn't that I was missing out, it was that something was literally missing from deep inside my soul. There was an emptiness. A spiritual bankruptcy, if you will.

The twists and turns of life led me down a path of questioning and seeking. This seemingly endless exploration led to years of doubts and more pain and suffering. I decided I was too smart to believe in fairytales and myths of a God that cared what happened to me. Trauma, divorce, alcoholism, and other setbacks had beat the idea of a benevolent God right out of me.

I moved about as far away as possible from those moments of prayer and connection to God that I had experienced as a child. I searched for contentment, self-confidence, and meaning in all the wrong places - new jobs, new scenery (I moved a dozen or more times in my 20s and 30s), new relationships, new cars, new apartments, new jewelry, clothes, booze, shopping, and exercise. I constantly chased unhealthy friendships and romantic relationships that further eroded my fragile self esteem.

Instead of feeling content, I often felt depressed, anxious, helpless, hopeless, and uninspired. In the end, everything felt pointless. I was a rudderless ship lost at sea relying on the unpredictable winds of this wild and often discouraging world to set my path. This was no way to live.

God, however, continually reached out to me in subtle and sometimes not so subtle ways. He tried for a long time to get my attention. Thirty years ago, my group of high school friends often ended up at a 24-hour Howard Johnson's diner for late-night grub. It was a five-minute walk from my house and had the best hot apple pie and ice cream. One night, however, I was in the mood for some actual food, so I ordered a chicken pot pie. A couple of minutes later the server informed me that they were all out of chicken pot pies so I would have to settle for something else.

At the time I received this update, my friends and I had been in a heated discussion about religion, so I offhandedly pleaded with God, "to please bring me a chicken pot pie!"

Then I obligingly changed my order. But about 30 seconds later, the server returned and happily informed me that someone had found a chicken pot pie in the back of the freezer.

Chapter 11

It's a funny story and completely inconsequential, but I know my Higher Power was at work and has a sense of humor. I can think back on many other examples: some serious - like walking away unscathed from a car wreck or a good samaritan finding my wallet outside a grocery store in a not-so-great part of town and turning it into security - and others more trivial - like getting the last seat of a crowded train. I responded in a similar way each time regardless of the scenario; I shrugged it off and moved on.

Unfortunately for me, I was one of the stubborn members of the flock. I ignored God's efforts to reach me for many, many years. I had to smack into some very low lows before I finally caught on.

But opening my mind to God and becoming willing to accept that maybe there was something at work was not what changed my life. My gateway to God and peace was prayer. It may sound obvious to some, but I was a novice when it came to matters of prayer and connection with a higher power. My approach to prayer had not evolved since the "Now I lay me down to sleep" days of childhood.

It's no secret that prayer can be a powerful force. A variety of studies extol the benefits of prayer, particularly on mental health. While the science of prayer's personal benefits is established, I have discovered that prayer itself is more of an artform than a science, and we each fashion an approach that works for us.

Prayer was always a last resort for me through my teens and well into adulthood. I prayed in my darkest moments, bargaining with God to save me from myself. I bargained with Him, "Please get me out of this mess, and I will never make this mistake again," or, "Please let me get this job, and I won't ask you for anything else… for a while."

I had confused God with Santa Claus or a Disney-movie genie who was going to grant me wishes without my needing to accept any responsibility, action, or accountability on my part. I was in for a rude awakening.

In a moment of complete surrender, I started to ask God what He wanted. I started to listen for answers and not just make demands. I launched a relationship with my Heavenly Father. I imagined Him just as that - a caring parent who wants the best for me. A guardian who looks out for me but has expectations for me too. I wanted Him in my life and that requires effort. Who wants a friend who only calls when they need something? How can God help if I don't listen or look for His will in my life?

The phrase "thoughts and prayers" has become a bit of a hollow statement and even a punchline in some circles, viewed as a throwaway term shared in response to the latest mass shooting, war, humanitarian crisis, natural disaster, or other tragic events that seem to come at us on a daily basis. Just as with my understanding of God, I also found prayer unfamiliar and confounding. What were people praying about? Did they really believe that they could pray for money and it would turn up? That God was sitting around listening for their specific request to come in?

I had so few examples in my life of genuine prayer. I have already mentioned my childhood bedtime "God Bless so and so" ritual. I also recited the basic dinnertime prayer at friends' houses ("God is good. God is great. Let us thank Him for the food we're about to eat. Amen.") I had heard church leaders say, "And let us pray," but everything they said after that sounded like a Biblical recitation of generic verse or general requests. This prayer wasn't for me. This prayer was for people who were not recovering from trauma, who weren't constantly bogged down by the weight of their failures, who had perfect lives and perfect families and no secrets to hide.

It wasn't until I viewed prayer as something completely different than a cut-and-paste solution or a recitation that it started to make sense to me. My journey from rote prayer to an ongoing conversation with God happened in stages.

One day years ago, a colleague - let's call her Chloe - entered my office while I was in the middle of a panic attack induced by yet another snippy, passive aggressive email from my micromanaging

Chapter 11

supervisor. I was well aware of her relationship with God and frankly envied her dedication and the peace she exuded. She was the perfect person to catch me at this moment. While I was on the verge of tears, she gently closed my office door and asked if we could pray together. Her request caught me off guard, but I welcomed her offer like she was handing out glasses during a solar eclipse.

I stepped out from behind my desk and linked hands with Chloe. We bowed our heads and she prayed over me in a calming, confident voice that washed over me like warm water on an icy day. The familiar terms she used to address her Higher Power and the simple requests she made for protection, comfort, and grace opened a new portal for me to prayer. It felt so personal and authentic. There was no bargaining or specific need or want outside of peace at that moment. And I felt it. I felt God in that room and my eyes became opened to a new way of communicating with my Higher Power.

I experienced another key turning point during a session with a mental toughness coach I had retained to help me develop better communication skills and build confidence. I had tried many avenues of finding peace and contentment and addressing my insecurities and fears. This was another piece of the puzzle.

In addition to his many qualifications, my coach Andrew also has a Ph.D. in Theological Studies. With my encouragement, Andrew often brought faith and God into our coaching activities. On more than one occasion, I unloaded about that former boss and their unreasonable expectations, and frankly unethical behaviors, they had subjected me to.

Andrew's suggestion was not what I expected. He advised me to pray for my former boss. "Pray that they have everything they want. That their life is perfect, from good health to a big bank account to a happy marriage. Heck, let's even ask God to make sure every blade of grass on their lawn is green and beautiful."

So that's how we dealt with my resentments toward my ex-boss and countless others I had been carrying around for years. It was another transformative moment. The message was twofold: 1. We are all spiritually sick and suffering and need help from a higher power. 2. Compassion is the antidote to resentment, as it frees up so much wasted energy and opens the door to serenity.

These experiences activated a feeling of grace that I had never before known. I learned the benefit of praying without expectation and the importance of inviting God into everything.

It's simple for me; I view prayer as talking to God, my heavenly dad, friend, and Holy guide through this wacky world. I bring Him my challenges. I tell Him about my fears. I ask Him for direction. I give Him my gratitude. I ask Him questions. And importantly, I also make time to listen. Some people consider this meditation. For me, it's sitting with God and letting Him know I am open to whatever His will may be. My God is a loving God with a great sense of humor, and I am sure to call Him out on His not-so-subtle nudges and ironies.

Sometimes I pray at a set time. For example, before bed I read from a daily devotional and have a conversation with God. Other times, I pray when I need comfort; instead of panicking when I am getting blood drawn or getting dental work done, or freaking out about a mistake I made, I talk to God. I ask Him to help me through the moment, to be with me. I tell Him I know that He's got this figured out.

Before God and I began this ongoing dialogue, I found myself calling my mom, my husband, a friend, or a coworker to dump all my anxiety and fear onto. There is certainly nothing wrong with discussing challenges or worries with friends and family, however. I find that when I connect with God, I am not simply there to vent or let my emotions out, I am there to find peace and comfort. I am demonstrating my faith, which gives me an incredibly empowering feeling.

Chapter 11

Here are a few more pointers for prayer:

- Pray for a person who you are upset with, in the middle of a fight with, or just plain don't like.
- When you tell someone that you'll pray for them, do it. Be specific.
- Ask a friend or even a stranger if there is something you can pray about on their behalf.
- Beginning and ending the day with prayer is great, but pray everywhere and anywhere.
- Don't overthink it. Start somewhere. Sometimes "God, help me" is enough.
- Consider sharing your gratitude with God by thanking your Higher Power in the moment.
- Make a "God Box" from an old shoe box that you decorate, or a special box that has meaning to you. Write down your worries and prayers and deposit them into the box. Have faith that God will listen and respond at the right time.

Every occasion is a reason to pray: before a big presentation, before a medical procedure, before a meal. And remember that prayers are not just requests, they are also expressions of gratitude. Talk to God after the big victory, after a safe flight, and after the job promotion.

Rather than gossip, pray. Rather than try to control, pray. Rather than worry, pray. As your Higher Power takes shape and becomes a part of your life, try to find venues for digging deeper and building a closer relationship with God, whether through a walk through the woods, meditation by the water, a discussion with like-minded people, or study through books, classes, films, or travel. Your Higher Power wants you to continue to nourish your spirituality, while all of the noise of the world works to disrupt and sever your connection to spirit.

You don't need to define your faith, adopt someone else's Higher Power, go to church, or take college classes, you just need to be open to exploring the idea of something greater than yourself, or greater than whatever is holding you down. Step away from right and wrong, church politics, and stereotypes to take a personal journey to find your higher power.

In surrendering to a higher power, I found freedom and peace. I could release resentments more quickly. I could see the good in situations. I could forgive others and myself for my divorce, not having shown up for people in the past, and manipulating others when I'd had no other tools to meet my needs.

I could begin making deposits into my spiritual account and begin to move from bankruptcy to bounty. Just like with any relationship, it takes time, and it ebbs and flows. It evolves and it grows. The more I give the more I receive. It requires discipline, obedience, and sacrifice.

Today I am at peace. I am hopeful. I am a victor, not a victim. Dare I say, I am content. I ask God to bless Erica each night and rest assured that someone is listening.

For reflection:

1. What is keeping you from realizing a genuine relationship with a Higher Power?
2. How do insecurities, addictions, and fear separate us from God?
3. For whom do you typically pray, and for what?
4. If God or a Higher Power exists, what type of life would He/Her/It want for you?

About the Author
Erica Hurtt

Erica Hurtt is a former Emmy-award-winning broadcast journalist and current blogger who writes about recovery, spirituality, parenthood, and raising goats. She also shares insights on Hawaiian culture through a "Mainlander" lens. In her darkest hours, she never imagined that trauma and mental health struggles would lead to beautiful discoveries, including finding God and her true self. When she is not writing, Erica can be found searching the beach for shells, sitting in a pasture with her goats, spending time with her family, or plotting her next travel adventure. Erica lives on a ranch on Hawaii's Big Island with her husband, daughter, and 18 goats, give or take a few. She has degrees in Communications and Journalism, and a college-level Certificate in Christian Ministry and Theology.

You can read more of her work here:
www.gobigislandorgohome.com

Chapter 12

Dancing With The Divine

Gina Jenkins

It's the year 2000, the music is thumping, the bass is pumping, and there you find me on the dance floor, fully aligned. Fast forward twenty plus years later, and you'll find me in a bathtub recording this chapter. My journey of Awakening Within truly began on the dance floor in my twenties. I found my long lost "twin flame;" this go-round, he likes boys. We met on an interview for United Airlines, the flight attendant position. We'd been flown to Chicago for the second round of interviews but didn't get asked to come back the next day for round three. Through deeply soulful conversation, he and I remembered somehow, subconsciously, that we knew each other. It was so familiar connecting with him. It was that night I discovered the gay dance club and how much I enjoyed and would seek after dancing among the boys who like boys, completely liberated, experiencing pure joy in my soul.

Now, twenty plus years later, I understand trauma, I understand brain science, I've been on a healing journey for some time. And my journey includes breaking free of some deeply programmed dogmatic teaching, as I was raised in the "Western Organized Religious Institute" that some still call the church. I subscribe to the belief that individuals are the church, but I digress. It was 2018, my nine-year marriage was quite volatile, depressing, confusing, dissatisfying, and disheartening. And I know I wasn't alone in those feelings. I acknowledge my then-husband had his own set of feelings and experiences that were quite less than ideal. We were nearing a separation. I knew that he was nearing his end and I was desperately looking for answers. A girlfriend had shared a healing modality within the church but outside the "normal bounds" that I had known as acceptable to a Christian and I was curious. I engaged in some "Heart-Sync" sessions, more of a spirit-led intercessory prayer type session, and my understanding of "me" being composed of different parts began to take shape.

You see, I had watched a Billy Graham special when I was four years old while still living with my mother and father. Their relationship was contentious, volatile, chaotic, and destructive. But in a moment of respite, I was sitting in front of the TV watching Billy Graham give a live presentation at some football stadium. I have a vivid memory of turning to my parents and asking them to help me "pray the prayer," invite Jesus into my heart. I have a vivid memory of being upstairs in my bedroom kneeling down on my little bed and "praying the prayer," asking Jesus into my heart. In the year 2021, those memories came flooding back and the Truth entered my consciousness: the Truth that it wasn't the dogmatic programming that I subscribed to and the many years of hypocrisy and discord that followed under the guise of a "Christian home." that I had responded to I now know I responded to the call of love, for that is what Yeshua is: the demonstration of Pure Love here in human form.

So in 2018, I was very much a church goer: I had been a leader in the church, I had led Bible studies, I had given many teachings, I had worked in the church office, I had subscribed to all the dogmatic programming 100%. I've since taken responsibility for how I've complicitly hurt others under that dogmatic programming. However, in the summer of 2018 I found myself in bed reading a book called, *Living From the Heart Jesus Gave You*. It came to me through the Heart-Sync sessions. I looked at the maturity indicators

Chapter 12

in the middle of the book that showed the brain maturation process that happens from infancy to adulthood.

I looked at the infancy chart and saw the listed adult behaviors toward infants that lead to a healthy brain, things like:

- being responded to
- knowing you're unique
- knowing your special
- knowing you're cared for
- knowing your needs are met

And then the last column in that chart showed what the adult's life looks like when those levels are not met, when developmental stages are not passed. My mouth literally hung open and I was overcome with awe, shock and shame all at the same time. I recognized my life and those words, and then thought, *O.M.G. that's what's wrong with me*, because I had experienced tremendous self-loathing most of my life.

You see, after that memory of praying the prayer in response to Billy Graham's altar call, my parents didn't stay together much longer and they split with a lot of chaos and discord. And a couple years later, a child custody battle ensued that left me incredibly traumatized. After being told I would have to choose who I wanted to live with, writing a letter to my mother to say I wanted to choose her and it being intercepted by my father, I was devastated on the custody hearing day. I was sitting outside the courtroom thinking I may be called in at any moment, then hugging my mother goodbye in the parking lot after she'd lost the case and was then moving out of state. I ended up living with my dad and step mom, being raised by them most of my childhood, and hearing how disturbed my mother was when she had become pregnant with me, how she didn't want me as a child, and that the doctor had to tell her when she was seven months pregnant that if she didn't change her attitude, she was going to lose me. I heard the stories. I listened and I didn't pay much attention or really take them to heart. But in 2018, as I looked at that maturity indicator chart, I understood what was "wrong with me" was that I had not attached properly as an infant or child. I then began a really deep healing journey. And the first real decision in mind that I made was to "trust the Lord with all my heart and lean not on my own understanding" and "in all my ways acknowledge Him," and I knew that if I did so, my path would straighten up. I knew that I couldn't go wrong, I knew that I could not lose. I trusted and I believed and I had faith. I made a decision to start surrendering - to open my hands up, release control, and surrender. Now for someone who at age 48 had known nothing but white-knuckle-gripped control from pretty much the crib, it's been a process. It has not been one and done, it has not been overnight; it has been layer by layer, glory to glory, day by day.

In November of 2018, my husband moved and out we separated for eight months. During that time, I cried all the tears. I buried myself in my bed and I went after my healing with a vengeance and tenacity. I was in a Journey Group at that point, meeting weekly with them learning brain science and growing myself up. I added other healing sessions, trying different modalities, and made progress. In July of 2019, my husband and I reunited on my birthday. We woke up together in the house I'm in now and I knew that I had been given a whole new lease on life. I began to live such an incredibly joyful life full of gratitude and thankfulness. I had learned how joy fuels the brain.

I had built an appreciation memory library for years. I had established an interactive Immanuel journaling exercise. I was confident. I was joyful. I was grateful. And for an entire year, my husband and I enjoyed peace. We walked our town night after night, talking and making what I thought was progress. In 2020 we all know we got locked down, and I'll tell you in 2020, when that happened in March, I knew it was an incredible opportunity to go even deeper in my faith. I had started to see some little tiny rumblings in my relationship with my husband, and there was some fear still there and insecurity that fleshed out later that year. That summer, right after we bought our house together and got a dog, we started fighting. Then during fall, because of lockdown, I got on social media and

Chapter 12

started finding out about the online world and the online business world.

In Fall 2020, I got into the Big Talk Academy with Trisha Brooke and wrote a speech on transforming narcissism, a total brain rewire. Because what I absolutely understood was that I had been stuck in infantile behavior, what many would call narcissistic behavior, which is one and the same. This behavior comes from the infant that wasn't cared for properly, so is constantly looking for validation and approval from outside sources. The infant/narcissist is always thinking that everything is a game that needs to be won. They are so insecure, in such self-protection mode that they do not see clearly. They do not think clearly, as they are looping in such incredible limitation and such insecurity, and typically there is a lot of trauma to clear off the DNA track. And having done that work, I have a real understanding of just what is possible when you go on the healing journey. In 2021, after I gave that speech with the Big Talk Academy, my husband moved out and separated from me again. The next month, he called for a divorce. I hired a life coach and she held my hand through that whole process. She helped see in me what I could not even quite see in myself yet. She started planting amazing seeds that led to my true Awakening that summer.

The Awakening Within came in a profound way that summer when I met Dr. Erin Fall Haskelll and joined her Soulciete. I began to hear about Universal Laws and metaphysics for the first time. My whole body responded when I first heard this information—my heart lit up, my soul lit up, and I knew I had come HOME. I knew I'd finally understand. My awakening came during an E4 trauma session while working with a coach, going back to what I call the "Golden Nugget" or "Holy Grail" memory of myself in a crib. One morning, while not being responded to, my cries went unanswered, I watched my mother's back in the kitchen the whole time, then fell back in the crib, gave up on life, and decided something was wrong with me, that my life wasn't worth living, and I realized how those threads have played out in my entire life up to this point.

And the most dramatic cementing of what I was learning occurred when I was returning home on an airplane from a trip to Oklahoma, meditating, listening to some music, journaling, and wanting to get clarity. I was asking Spirit to truly make it clear to me if I was to stay with Soulciete, which would really be breaking away from dogmatic programming, really breaking away from the W.O.R.I., who still want to put God and Jesus outside. They want to continue keeping God as some big man up in the sky and Jesus as supposedly coming out of your heart and getting on a cloud to come "back" and save you, and that is not the Truth. And I was at a crossroads because that's what I had grown up hearing and believing my entire life up to this point. So there I was in the airplane asking for clarity, and what came through was incredible. Knowing that my experience of the Immanuel lifestyle is believing God is with me, it was incredibly easy to begin to see God within me. Nothing separates me from Love, nothing; of course I am Love. Of course that's what people see in me, of course! And so in that airplane it dropped in that if we all got how to embody our faith, to this point, that we woke all the way up to our Divinity and knew we could maintain peace as our baseline all the time, then of course we the people would become that City on the Hill shining so bright. Of course it's the people, and as it dropped into my soul so deeply, the airplane literally dropped in the sky. I did not make that up. That was it for me!

I don't look back because from that place of gaining that confidence to continue moving forward in this new direction, life has only continued to perfectly unfold. I have since become certified as a Spiritual Practitioner, as a Spiritual Psychology Coach, and as a Radical Recovery Coach. I have such a deep understanding now of not only the brain science, but the metaphysics and the spirituality of this entire experience, and the creative process, and looking at the Bible as the allegorical writing that it is. Everything has opened up incredibly for me. I am so deeply and intimately connected with the Infinite Intelligence in which I move and breathe and have my being that some still want to call God, and it is fine. Because what I absolutely know after studying world religions within the ministerial

Chapter 12

program is that every single religion wants to put a name on this nameless substance that Quantum science has found which has caught up with the ancient wisdom. We want to name it but it is nameless, it is Infinite Intelligence that we move and breathe and have our being in, and we want to think this is air we are breathing in, but it is more. The truth is we are powerful creators creating our reality with our beliefs, thoughts, emotions, and words.

And so awakening within has become a dance once again for me on this spiritual dance floor with the Divine. I am getting used to the Divinity Within Me leading and guiding this dance. I am getting out of my own way more and more and more and more, and getting ready to take the Radical Recovery of the Divine Self message out into the world on public stages. I know and believe that my words are law and that I can manifest anything that I truly desire that lines up with my purpose of being here. I see my transformation and I know that I'm here to show others what is possible. What is possible in life is that you pick your Journey as you come back into this lifetime, your parents, and your lessons, and I didn't get that a long time ago. These were new concepts for me in 2021, and it took me some time to fully embody these Truths. I had to cut my birth mother off for two and a half years to truly dive deep within and clear that trauma off my DNA tracks and come to full forgiveness of her and myself. I understand that I must go pick that little baby girl up from the crib when I'm triggered and remind her that nothing is wrong with her. I don't look to my mother to do that for me because she cannot, and I accept that. I have deep compassion for her and we have this amazing grace-filled relationship today that is an absolute miracle. It is the fruit of completely surrendering to the dance with the divine.

About the Author
Gina Jenkins

Reverend Gina Jenkins is an author, spiritual leader, and motivational speaker delivering a powerfully transformative message about Radical Responsibility. She is the founder of She Incorporates, where she offers several modalities for trauma healing and subconscious reprogramming. Her message is that through radical recovery of the Divine Self, we can eradicate codependency and narcissism from our lives.

Gina resides on the Central Coast of California with two of her three children, a small dog, and 3 cats. She enjoys gardening and teaching barre, sculpt and yoga classes locally and online.

Connect with Gina:
Instagram -@revginaj
Facebook - @gigijenkins
LinkedIn- @GinaJenkins

Chapter 13

A Journey to Purpose: On the Wings of Community

Glenda Sheard

 "You will get to know yourself the most during the hardest times. But you probably won't recognize this until hindsight."

~ Stacie Martin ~

Have you ever heard that eventually, as we get older, we become our parents? Who believes that when you are growing up? I remember hearing those words, but I was sure that would never happen to me! My relationship with my mother had been immensely challenging when I was an all-knowing teenager and young adult. Looking back, I realize my mom was the most influential mentor and teacher I would ever have.

As a small child, I had no idea the incredible influence my mother's words of wisdom would have on me. She always emphasized the importance of helping others and positively impacting the world. From an early age, she instilled in me the value of volunteering and giving back. In my mother's words, *"Glenda, when you give your time freely to your community or a cause important to you, there are great opportunities to make a difference for others. You will also learn new things, grow your skills, and make lifelong friends. When we are helping others, we forget about our prob-*

lems. *And always remember, giving your time to your community is like recycling love."*

My mother had indeed planted a seed. I did not realize until later in my adult journey that her wisdom would help save my life.

As a child, I stored my mother's words in my memory bank but did not begin to understand their significance until I became an adult. And just like my mother had said, I started to genuinely appreciate her words of wisdom even more when I became a mom and gave back as a volunteer to our community. I soon realized that community involvement benefited those we helped and brought a sense of purpose and fulfillment to our lives. Whether volunteering at my son's school, a local soup kitchen, mentoring a child, or organizing a charity event, there were countless ways to influence the lives of others.

Growing up as a city kid, I had little exposure to farming or, as I called it, "that agriculture stuff." I had yet to learn how agriculture would play a role later in my life. There is one childhood experience I still laugh about today. Our family visited my cousins, who lived on a farm. I learned so much about living on a farm. We saw the farm animals, collected eggs from the chicken coop, took meals to the workers in the field, and jumped from the haystack in the barn. My cousins had cautioned me about putting the eggs in the pockets of my jeans. While jumping from the haystack, I learned about their cautionary words of wisdom. My mom also had insight because she had brought along extra clothes into which I could change. Also, I still remember the swat I received on my backside for not listening to my cousins and wasting freshly collected eggs.

Wise lessons:

Listening to someone with experience who knows much more about something than I do is an important skill. I call this listening louder.

Never put fresh eggs in your pockets.

I had begged my parents for a horse my entire childhood. My parents repeatedly explained that our family could not afford a

Chapter 13

horse; we lived in the city and knew nothing about horse ownership. It was an adventure I could take on as an adult. Whenever I heard the words "when you become an adult," I promised myself I would never say those words to my child when I became a parent. Since then, I have often laughed about this so-called wisdom I had as a teenager. Yes, I later often said those exact words to my son!

When I became an adult, my partner and I decided to purchase a home in a rural area with the consideration of owning a horse. Can you imagine how ecstatic I was when we learned that the neighbours across the road from our property owned show horses and racehorses? We quickly became friends, and they promised to teach me the ropes about being a responsible horse owner. A miracle happened soon after our move to the acreage. A colleague offered me a thoroughbred horse that was retiring from the racetrack! I was over the moon but had little knowledge about the journey I was about to embark on. "That agriculture stuff" became a reality! I will forever and a day be grateful for my neighbours, the horse community, and the 4H kids who taught me their motto, "Learn to do by doing." It certainly fits with the values my parents had instilled in me as a child: Learn, grow, fall, get up, keep going, never stop learning, and never give up. For the next eighteen years, my horse Smiley taught me similar values, and that animals often offer us more perspective and wisdom than humans. Also with the neighbours' encouragement, I signed up as a volunteer for an agricultural organization. I could have never imagined then that over thirty-five years later, I would be actively involved as a volunteer in rodeo and farming events and continue to benefit from "that agriculture stuff."

Wise Lessons:

Being a responsible pet owner requires patience and commitment.

Animals can offer unconditional love while at the same time trying our patience.

To take responsible risks.

To learn to do by doing is valuable wisdom for life.

Being a part of a community is a gift to treasure.

Always research before jumping into an idea!

Horses can be costly to own.

Our parents knew far more than we ever gave them credit for when we were younger.

We can do more when we become adults. Yet, as adults, we often reflect upon how much fun it was to be a kid.

When my son attended elementary school and began to play sports, the journey to becoming a committed volunteer truly began. I could have never imagined then that helping a small child to read at school would be just the beginning of volunteering with junior high and University students. Years later, I joined Toastmasters to enhance my public speaking and leadership skills. As part of the Toastmasters program, there were opportunities to teach junior high students communication and leadership skills. After four terms of teaching junior high students, I was proud to be able to take my communication and leadership skills to the next level. I served as a university and college instructor for over ten years. Teaching students communication and leadership skills is one of the major highlights of my giving back and allowed me to confidently enhance my skills as a mentor, communicator, and leader.

Wise lessons:

We can do anything when we learn new skills and believe in ourselves.

As the old saying goes, gifts are meant to be shared. Our talent and creativity can be fuel for others.

Chapter 13

 "I loved the Boy with the utmost love of which my soul is capable, and he is taken from me—yet in the agony of my spirit in surrendering such a treasure, I feel a thousand times richer than if I had never possessed it."

~ Willam Woodsworth ~

We were living life like most people were living. Up, down, good, bad, happy, and busy, and so life continued until everything changed!

My son passed away at age 21, and the person known as Darrel's Mom died too. A heartbroken shell of a woman was left behind. That woman was me. Being broken is part of the human experience, but losing my only child was beyond the darkest of nightmares! Becoming a mom was the most significant and treasured gift of my life. How could I go on now? How could I live without my son? After my son passed, I struggled with major depression and post-traumatic stress and felt I no longer had anything to live for. My purpose had died with my son. Everything had changed, and I was still living. How could it be? A couple of former friends no longer welcomed me into their lives, which may have been because they could not deal with my loss or grief. Others did their best to offer love and support, and a community began surrounding me. The hearts of support from friends and my community were everything I needed but did not have the strength to ask for. I knew it was essential to seek help from others and that I did not have to go through the loss of my son alone, but I was lost, feeling hopeless, shattered, and broken. How could I still be a mom when my only child had died?

As I continued to navigate through grief, I slowly learned that healing was a journey and opportunity for growth, but it would take time. A life of time. In my case, I was sure I would never heal, and that time only made grief different, not easier, as some people may believe. I also learned that grief is like a fingerprint, unique and different for every person who experiences the loss of a loved one. At a crossroads, I questioned everything: my existence, values, and what was enormously influential in life. It was the beginning of learning to take one moment at a time, give myself grace when needed, and find the courage to believe I still had a purpose.

In my circle of support, a friend suggested that writing in a journal might help me with my grief. I filled hundreds and hundreds of pages of journals, searching for hope and a reason to live. I wrote about how I loved and missed my son, the pain of losing him, and the kaleidoscope of emotions a person experiences when they lose a loved one. Another friend suggested that I start a gratitude journal. My son had died, and I did not feel there was anything to be grateful for any longer. After a slow start on a gratitude journal, I began to write about how fortunate I was to have had a child and that I was still a mom. A Mom to an Angel. Those were baby steps toward expressing gratitude and searching for purpose and hope.

It was nearly one year later before I considered volunteering again. I was afraid I no longer had anything to offer. In my grief, I had wondered if my passion for giving back had died with that other version of myself. I was also distraught at the idea that the post-traumatic stress I was struggling with could creep up at any moment without warning. I did not know how I might react if my trauma triggered me or what others would think if I experienced a flashback. Two questions pounded my thoughts and lay heavy on my heart: Would I remember any valuable skills I learned while actively involved in the community? And how would I manage an anxiety attack or flashback if it happened while I was volunteering? I was terrified, yet I knew I needed to find my place in the world where I belonged - more baby steps in the search for purpose and hope.

There will never be words that truly express my immense gratitude to the friends, colleagues and fellow volunteers who held my hand and heart as I eased myself back into volunteering. These caring people believed in me and seemed to know the passion to give back was still within me. I was the one that needed to believe. I knew I would always be my son's mom, and his legacy would live on in me. I was vulnerable yet hell-bent on living with passion and purpose again.

Chapter 13

An army of champions and cheerleaders were beside me, and a community that needed my support. The journey to rebuild myself began, one volunteer shift and community event at a time. My passion for giving back and community involvement seemed even more robust than I could remember. Before long, I was taking on leadership roles again like I had in the past. Whether sitting on an organizing committee for a significant event or working on smaller volunteer projects, I felt ignited and knew the spark had come back. I was a woman on a mission. It was a feeling of belonging, safe and comfortable, like returning to visit a trusted friend. I realized I still wore my heart on my sleeve, which was one of my most important strengths. I had a more profound sense of empathy for others, and I listened more intently. I always started and ended my day with gratitude. I regained confidence in my skills and knew it was the beginning of becoming a better me. I needed to feel my son would be proud of his mom.

My search to feel purpose again has been a difficult journey, and I still wonder how I have made it to this day. The sadness in my heart eases when I reflect upon the people who have been there for me on my darkest days and believed in me when I did not want to be here. Over the years, friends have told me, "I don't know if I could go on if my child died." I still want to scream at that statement sometimes; what choice do I have? Instead, I remind them of the tears and hugs we shared, the lengthy conversations and late-night calls offering me their love and support, and how they held me up when I was unsure if I could go on. I also remind myself of how far I have come.

Then there are friends and fellow volunteers who have never met my son and only know him through the stories I share. They listened, always wanting to hear the stories again. Those same friends sense when I am feeling down and reach out to me with compassion and kindness. Then there are the kind-hearted friends who always remember the date of my son's birthday and the anniversary of his passing. I call these friends earth angels.

Wise lessons:

We are braver than we think and stronger than we realize.

We do not have to understand what someone is going through to be supportive and show them kindness and compassion.

We can live through trials, tribulations, and tragedies by reaching out to people who care about us.

Anyone can experience mental health challenges. There is help if you do.

We experience growth even when we may be feeling hopeless.

The most essential part of communication is listening.

The best thing to say when we do not know what to say is, I am deeply sorry for your loss. I am here for you.

Being an altruistic person gives a sense of pride.

Life is full of choices. Choose wisely.

A gratitude attitude will contribute significantly to your life and the lives surrounding you.

The wisdom I have shared does not always come from giving back to your community, but it is wisdom to take wherever you go.

Everyone has days and times that are hard. On those days, I reflect most on my mother's words, *"When we give back, we forget about our problems."* I have become more resilient by getting out of bed on the hard days when I want to hide under the covers. I have learned how smiling at a stranger while volunteering can transform a lousy day into a better one. We never know what another person may be going through and how a simple act of kindness can positively change the day for both the giver and the receiver. I know my mom intended to empower me to make the best of every day while living to positively impact the lives of others and the community.

Muhammad Ali said, *"Service to others is the rent you pay for your room here on earth."* Volunteering and community involvement are essential for

Chapter 13

positively impacting the world and making a difference in the lives of others. My mother instilled these values in me, and I strive to live by her example every day. I will forever be grateful for her wisdom and guidance, and proud to carry her compassion and legacy of community involvement. My mom and I were immensely proud of my son when he started his path of volunteering by coaching a girls' baseball team in our community. He often teased us, saying, "My baba made me do it, and so did my mom." We would all laugh, knowing we were volunteers because we wanted to be. I encourage everyone to freely give their time to a cause that is important to them. It can be life-changing, or even lifesaving, while making a difference for others. I received more than I could have ever asked for on my journey toward purpose on the wings of the community. Like my mom said, *"Giving back to one's community is just like recycling love."*

 " The best way to find yourself is to lose yourself in the service of others."

~Mahatma Gandhi~

About the Author
Glenda Sheard

Glenda Sheard is a radio talk show host, motivational speaker, author, and public speaking coach. She is a multi-dimensional entrepreneur and mentor whose goal is to help community leaders listen louder, connect with intention, and communicate with empathy. Glenda is grateful to have experienced success as a member of the media, a fundraising professional, and an entrepreneur.

Life hasn't always been kind to Glenda; she has lived with adversity, loss, and despair. There is no greater tragedy or trauma than losing her only child. Her journey to carry on as Darrel's Mom has been taken one step and one breath at a time.

On her journey, she never lost sight of the importance of community, gratitude, authenticity, and learning to purposefully move forward. Glenda's immeasurable passion for community and volunteerism played a massive part in helping her live with purpose while making a difference for others and sharing her son's legacy whenever possible.

To connect with Glenda, visit:
https://linktr.ee/glendasheard

Chapter 14

Ambition to Authenticity: Rediscovering Myself on the Path to Empowerment

Taylor A. Caruthers

Have you ever found yourself chasing dreams, accomplishments, and success only to wake up one day feeling like a stranger in your own life? Crazy, right?! Well, being born in Merrillville, Indiana, and growing up in the South Suburbs of Chicago, there was something about the hustle and bustle of the Big City being so close but so far away that bred something in me that became ingrained in my DNA and set the tone for my life. I got my start in the Midwest, as did so many others in a super normal middle-class God-Fearing family, and along with that, I was the baby for a long time; everyone's baby, I might add. Going to church and Bible study were staples in my life. I was super spoiled, super smart, and surprisingly good at everything I put my mind to when it came to academics and sports. I always had the support and encouragement of my family to go more, do more, and be the best that I could despite anything. I was incredibly loved and cared for in all the ways my family best knew how to love and care for a child, but regardless, the he way I chose to move in my life, trying to figure things out on my own and thinking I wanted to be an adult when of course I had no idea what I was doing, led to me becoming pregnant at 15 years old! Despite ALL the things parents do to prevent something like that from happening; it still happened. I thought, Is my life over? Where do I go from here? What now? Conversations about parenting, abortion, and adoption were had, and how does a child have the ability to make such a powerful lifelong decision, let alone become a parent?!

Well for me, it looked like moving to western New York and having my child with the goal of finishing high school and going to college. At 16, and a single parent I started my junior year of high school, feeling very scattered but still very determined to live my best life, whatever that may be. Thankfully I was not isolated and didn't have to go to a special school and be publicly ostracized, as this was 2002, but the fear was real, and the adjustment was real. I had an incredibly dedicated support system, but while I was encouraged and taught how to be a mother, I also had the full responsibility of taking care of my child, going to school, getting good grades, and staying out of trouble. As expected, I was better at some of those than others. Essentially none of the rules changed; I was not automatically granted adult privileges because I now had a child. I was a child with a child, and it was so hard to figure out who I really was in all of that. I successfully finished high school and graduated in 2004; not with all the grace and ease that I had originally planned, but resilient nonetheless. It was an accomplishment not only because it was expected but because I did it with my almost 2-year-old watching me cross the stage and continue to move forward in life and not be defeated by my circumstances.

By all means of society, I should have been a statistic. A young black girl with a kid at 15 has the potential to essentially do nothing with her life but end up on government assistance and live a meager existence. I am here because this is NOT my story, nor does it have to be anyone else's. After graduation, I managed to still earn acceptance to multiple colleges, had the full support to go away to college, and live that dream, but I made the choice to attend a local community college to be a full-time parent and college student as a young adult. All sounds good but as young adults do, I continued to try

Chapter 14

doing this life thing without the fundamental understanding that life is going to life you every which way, and you must be prepared for the ups and downs as they flow.

So, my life goes as such: I had my first born at age 15, my second at 19, my third at 21, and my fourth at 23. In the midst of bringing new life into the world, I was still trying to build my own. Once I figured out that the traditional college route wasn't for me and that my dream of being a broadcast journalist would possibly take too long to accomplish, I decided I wanted a stable career I would enjoy, and a career in healthcare made the most sense. Therefore, I began the rigorous process of applying to and finally getting into nursing school. I was the youngest in my practical nursing class. I graduated in 2008, took my boards and obtained my license in early 2009, and never looked back. Prior to working in healthcare, I had been building a solid career in customer service and sales, and I took that knowledge forward into my nursing career. I was wired to work hard, go hard, do more, and be better, so I was always the young lady with ambition and drive, never content and never standing still. I landed some amazing opportunities early on in my healthcare career that allowed me to infuse and grow my business knowledge into the compassion and knowledge of being a nurse. This became the core of who I was and how I showed up in the world, and it caused me to excel in most environments! With some excellent mentorship and leadership training, I ascended the ranks over the years and this young black girl became a boss in every sense of the word. I had the titles, the salaries, the benefits, the life that appeared great.

What I didn't know and what others around me couldn't see was that I was moving so fast that I never stopped to feel! I didn't even realize how disassociated I had become from myself, let alone from those I loved. I did all the things I knew to do; I had a regular physical and mental health care regime which was very operational, functional, and practical. I was too smart for my own good. I felt comfortable there in my head, solving problems and coming up with solutions for complexities. It was all I knew. I just moved right along doing the next indicated thing, progressing to the next opportunity, and was never really present or even had a thought in my mind that something was off.

Like for most in the world, my life came crashing down in March of 2020 when we entered the phase of the global pandemic. I became surrounded by my husband and children 24/7, was running a business from home, and was gasping for air with no idea why. This caused me to spiral, to do everything besides look inward because nobody could tell me that anything was even wrong with me. However, the well-put-together, figure-it-out person had no solution. Like most people do, I sought solutions with unhealthy coping mechanisms. It almost killed me. Over time, I became unrecognizable to my family, friends, and most importantly, ME. There I was, 35 years old with all those accomplishments and a stellar resume, yet empty inside with no clue who I was. Doing and feeling are two very different things, and I existed in a realm that was never going to get me the success I thought I wanted and needed in my life because I was empty, running on fumes while the car sputtered and rolled to a stop.

Something had to change. Actually, everything! If it hadn't, I don't even know that I would even be here writing this today. The definition of insanity is to do something over and over expecting a different result. What I couldn't see then is that every day of my life had been riddled with insanity, one crazy decision after the next. Some call it rock bottom, and I relate to that, but the feeling of rock bottom felt higher than what I experienced, and it was absolutely terrifying, as well as lonely. It was time for me to step out of the insanity and do something sane, although it didn't feel like it or seem that way at the moment.

I moved across the country, sought professional help, and made a decision for ME for the first time ever to look inward, process, and heal in order to really move forward in my life. This is sometimes referred to as slowing down to speed up. I needed a full pause and reset because everything that was me worked incredibly well until it just didn't. While I struggled to grasp at the life I had and the

Chapter 14

dreams I thought were mine, I could not see myself in the picture. My only choice was to fully surrender my life to God and start making decisions that felt good to me, or die. No more drama for me whatsoever. And yes, I said *felt*, as in, *feel*, something I needed to learn how to do as an adult. It wasn't pretty and it wasn't perfect, but I had to choose ME regardless of how that seemed to anyone else. I had to minimize my need for outside validation in order to willingly come to the decision to choose me. I knew that my undying servitude of helping others could no longer be sustained if I did not serve myself first. I had poured from an empty cup for so many years that I couldn't even count them. I needed to be broken down, for what I now understand, was to build me back up in the capacity of who I truly am and what my soul was brought here to do. A quote someone shared with me early on my healing journey is: "Religion is for people who are afraid of Hell; spirituality is for those that have already been there."

The first time I heard about breathwork was in August of 2022 and my facilitator for this experience gave me and a few other ladies a quick rundown of possible effects that we could experience both physically and emotionally and me being the cynical and practical person that I am thought he was full of crap but again in this moment of surrender and experience I was kind of like whatever, I am here so might as well give it a shot. The thought of having this experience was a little scary and it didn't quite make sense, but I have leaned into the "Do it anyway" mentality. I set an intention to let go of hurt, pain, and anger and laid down to breathe. Within the first 30 seconds, I found myself crying intensely in a way where it wasn't just your normal cry, it was my soul coming out through my tears. As the session continued, I was tense throughout my body, I had spasms, ALL the things. I was a pile of mush on the floor at the end and it was the safest and seen I had felt probably in my entire life. Once I collected myself, I immediately approached the facilitator and told him that I found what my heart was missing, and I wanted to know if he could teach me how to bring it to others. He was so kind and gracious that he shared a ton of resources and my love for Breathwork was born out of my own experience and connection and my desire to bring this power to others. I eventually sought out and got trained by one of the best in the country. In that journey to obtain that certificate I learned so much more about myself and I also learned that my certificate meant nothing. The most important thing I can do is to keep showing up for myself and growing my capacity to show up for others. Hence the reason I believe that you can not take anyone to depths that you haven't gone yourself. Breathwork opened me up to be able to be present in my body, honor my feelings, and process my trauma amongst so many other benefits that it truly offers. This openness allowed me to receive Theta Healing and Reiki because it was like the door had finally been knocked down and I was finally ready to see and experience what else was out there!

I had to learn the basics: Who am I? What do I like to do? What is my favorite color? What are my hobbies? So simple that it hurt my brain to feed into what I thought was trivial, but I had no other solution to offer, so I was finally ready to listen, absorb, and implement. This is what radical acceptance looked like for me—learning and deciding that I am a master creator and I get to determine who I am. I get to create my reality. The power in those words brings me chills even to this moment. That same power and decisions are yours too if you choose to accept the challenge as well. I chose to accept the challenge. I finally decided that I was worth liking, loving, and fighting for. I finally decided that I needed to fight just as hard for myself as I had fought for so many other "things" in my life. I could have fallen by the wayside at age 15 and never given myself a chance, but that's not what I am here to do. I am the way maker; I am the generational curse breaker. I am my ancestors' wildest dreams.

Embracing healing modalities has served me in being able to handle life on life's terms and excel. Using a feelings wheel to decide what I was feeling and stop beating myself up for not necessarily having an explanation for why I was feeling it at that moment. Offering myself compassion. My feelings are valid. No matter how big or small, they all matter, and I do not owe the world or myself any explanation for

Chapter 14

what comes up in this human experience. I had to give myself the permission that the world hadn't openly given me. Imposter Syndrome is real. I am a young black woman growing more powerful and soulful each and every day; not because of the position that I hold with my employer, and not because I am a CEO of my own company, but simply because I am me, unapologetically and truly. I was told a long time ago that you take yourself with you wherever you go, and I am finally proud of who I am, so I take her with me into every interaction. I live from a place of love and compassion, not anxiety and haste. I have perspective when I interact with others. I get to choose my reaction 100% of the time. I can see what has happened *for* me in my life and not *to* me. My journey is far from over; this is just the beginning.

I feel honored to be able to show up as me in a coaching and healing capacity, creating more diversity and access in hopes of encouraging others to do more of the same. Many years ago, my brother in law asked me a simple question, "Hey sis, what are we doing today?" My response: "Trying to take over the world!" Little did I know that that was really what I am here to do. Maybe not in the form of world domination, but rather through using my voice, sharing my story, and challenging the status quo. I am no longer playing small; I am here to claim my space and create change through impact and legacy, through my very own unique authenticity, showing, doing and holding the door open for those who are curious about evolving and awakening without trials and tribulations. I am eternally grateful for my every trial and every tribulation because they have served me to be here with you right now at this moment. We are exactly where we are supposed to be when we are supposed to be there! Always remember that and stay true to you, no matter what!

About the Author
Taylor A. Caruthers

Taylor Caruthers is a mother of five who has conquered the odds. She embraced motherhood at age 15, determined to graduate high school and create a better future for herself. While navigating a predominantly white workplace as a young woman of color, she pursued her passion for nursing and relentlessly climbed the career ladder.

Through life's trials, Taylor discovered the transformative power of authenticity and healing. With fourteen years of nursing experience, she now serves at a renowned reproductive health organization. Taylor creates a safe space for others, enhanced by her personal journey, expertise in life coaching, breathwork, and knowledge of Theta Healing.

Taylor's approach to coaching, business and life in general emphasizes anti-racism, gender inclusivity, and trauma-informed care. Taylor believes in the beauty of individuality, which echoes her mentor's wisdom: "People are where they are when they are there!" She's ready to meet you where you are. She embodies the strength that arises from embracing authenticity. In a world that often molds us, Taylor's story inspires us to celebrate our unique paths.

Connect with Taylor:

FB: https://www.facebook.com/taylor.a.caruthers/
IG: https://www.instagram.com/metanoia_innovative_solutions/
Website:
https://www.metanoiainnovativesolutions.com

Thank you

Thank you for reading and coming along with all of us on our journeys as we learned how to open our eyes a little wider and follow our inner wisdom to transform the way we live our lives.

We hope you enjoyed this book and perhaps have re-ignited that spark within yourself to connect to and nurture as you follow your own path of discovery.

Authors of Awakening the Power Within

Inspired Hearts
Publishing

Inspired Hearts Publishing is passionate about sharing inspiring stories of men and women who've overcome great hardships, experienced untraditional success, and are carving out their own path in life—stories of hope, inspiration, strength, resilience, love, and transformation.

We thrive on providing a platform for business owners to leverage their personal story, experience, and expertise to grow their audience and establish themselves as an expert in their industry.

If you loved this book, please give us a 5 star review on Amazon or GoodReads
and
Send us an email at write@inspiredheartspublishing.com.

Manufactured by Amazon.ca
Bolton, ON